Marksm
Coaching

Front Cover
Queen's Medal and Bars (J Alexander)
NRA Medal and Bars (R O'Neill), NPA Medal and Bars (R Jeffries)
Sig Sauer Pistol and Accuracy International Rifle
This Page
Additional medals shown by kind permission of J Alexander and R Jeffries

© World Copyright 1996 Ray O'Neill
and
S&S Systems

First Edition - March 1996

Published by

S&S Systems, Bretton Court, Manor Road
Wales Village, Sheffield, S31 8PD, England
Tel: (01909) 773399 • Fax: (01909) 773645 • International Code: (+44 1909)

constantia et aequum cum flexione proba

British Library Cataloguing in Publication Data:
O'Neill, Ray, 1946 -
Marksmanship Coaching
A catalogue record for this book is available from the British Library

ISBN 0-95244-740-1

Printed and Bound in Great Britain by Cox and Wyman Ltd, Reading, England

Dedicated to my late twin brother

Ken

1946 - 1968

Contents

List of Illustrations

Acknowledgements

My thanks go to Woody and Baz for their practical advice and in-house training and to all those firers and coaches who have, over the years, demonstrated and explained their marksmanship techniques; their names would fill this book.

I would like to record my appreciation to Lt Col Hodges, Lt Col Thomas and Lt Col Hastings for their encouragement and for allowing me the opportunity to confirm the techniques described in my book with numerous firing exercises during range work over the last ten years.

I would also like to thank D Dodd (Gunsmith and Firearms Restorer), B James (Armourer), G Atkinson and M Ward (Photographers) for their assistance, and Maj B Robertshaw for some of the drawings and illustrations.

Thanks also to Capt J Alexander (fours times Queen's Medal and Service Rifle), Sgt Maj B Kelly (Master Sniper, Warminster), M Shehan and M Upton (BG Instructors), R Jeffries (Great Britain Service and Police Pistol Team), Sgt Maj R Harrison (Specialist Training Team), R Malbon (NRA, RCO), I Leedham (South Yorkshire Police Firearms Licensing Shooting Team, British Practical Rifle Champion, 1995) and Curtis L Wood (Vietnam and Gulf War Veteran) for their proof reading and valuable comments.

Finally, my special thanks to Stephen and Susan Alsop for taking my notes and sketches and producing this book at S&S Systems.

Ray O'Neill
England

March 1996

Foreword

I first met the author when I was appointed Chief Instructor to a Specialist Skill at Arms Training Team.

His appointment was Master Coach, responsible for training Range Conducting Officers and Coaches on all types of ranges, including Individual Close Quarter Battle and Team Battle shooting ranges, using handguns, sub machine guns, sniper rifles and GPMG/SA80 in the air defence role.

He is a School of Infantry (Warminster) qualified Range Conducting Officer and Support Weapons Wing trained Mortar Fire Controller, School of Artillery qualified, All Arms Air Defence Instructor and a National Rifle Association fully qualified Range Conducting Officer and Service Pistol Coach.

Before joining the training team he was the Weapon Training Warrant Officer with an Infantry Battalion and also found the time to be a Ministry of Defence Deer Stalker.

He gained immense experience of competition shooting as a competitor, coach and Bisley Team Captain with team members winning the Queen's Medal (Service Rifle) Sub Machine Gun and Service Pistol Championships.

He has represented Great Britain in International Skill at Arms matches against American, Australian, Canadian, South African, Danish, Dutch, French, German and Italian armed forces personnel. His personal shooting achievements include:

National Rifle Association Medal and Bars for:

Service Rifle
Sub Machine Gun Cup
Service Pistol Cup

National Pistol Association Medal with Gold, Silver, Bronze Oak Leaf Clusters for:

Service Pistol
Police Pistol
Practical Pistol

United States Armed Forces Skill at Arms Meeting:

National Match Pistol, Excellence in Competition, Highest Score, Allied International Competitor.

In 1980, whilst shooting in the United States of America, he was consultant to a firearms dealer, advising on the types of handgun to be imported into the United Kingdom due to the growing interest in action shooting events. This subsequently led to him being credited with introducing the Northern Region Police, Service and Action Shooting Championships that has attracted competitors, spectators and sponsors to the sport.

His present duties include coaching and assessing service personnel, including prospective candidates for special forces. He also coaches body guard personnel in the use of handguns for close protection in countries where this is legally permitted.

His practical knowledge of shooting, coaching and range work gained over 35 years is more than apparent in this book. It must be the definitive aide-mémoire for all those who aspire to coach and shoot quickly and accurately.

Over the years it has been my privilege to meet and work with many skill at arms specialists and experts at handgun shooting - I have never met a better one than Ray O'Neill.

Major K Steel, SAS (Retired)
January 1996

Introduction

The handgun was originally designed to be fired using one hand. The firer was, as is still the case, coached to use the classic Duelling Stance, to present as narrow a target as possible to an opponent. With the introduction of body armour it was accepted that it was more practical to face an opponent squarely than to present an open side.

Action Shooting disciplines have gained in popularity, making it necessary for coaching and shooting techniques to change, to enable targets to be engaged quickly and accurately.

My aim is to give an introduction to the techniques that have to be mastered to become a proficient firer and to provide the coach with the information to plan an interesting and progressive shooting programme with the aim of building confidence and shooting skill.

In theory, a sound knowledge of shooting can be gained from reading, but shooting skill can only be achieved by good coaching and shooting practise. Each stage must be mastered before progressing onto the next.

The art of Coaching is to pass on information gained from experiences and to offer encouragement whilst correcting any errors in the firer's technique.

The coach must have a sound knowledge of shooting and, ideally, personal shooting ability. He must be able to advise, demonstrate and correct faults in the firer's techniques and be totally familiar with the range safety rules and the safe handling of firearms.

There is nothing difficult about shooting a handgun quickly and accurately:

When drawing from the holster, ensure that the **grip is correct** and that the **stable position adopted** enables the handgun to **point naturally** at the target. On coming up into the aim, concentrate on the **sight picture** whilst **controlling breathing** and **squeeze the trigger to release the shot.**

Individual firers need only to confirm, by firing, which of the co-ordinated techniques gives them the consistency to shoot well.

In the UK, civilians are not permitted to own centre fire self loading or pump action rifles. This has led to an increase in interest in some of the original repeating firearms, particularly those that share the same ammunition as the handgun. I have therefore included a chapter giving a brief history of their development, safe handling and coaching information together with the sharp shooting skills for practical rifle.

For simplicity in writing, I have referred to the firer as 'he' rather than 'she'. The techniques I have described enable any individual to compete on equal terms, irrespective of build and whether right or left handed.

The number of firearms illustrated are restricted by space. The fact that I have omitted to show other firearms does not infer that they are any less reliable or accurate.

All measurements are approximate and drawings are not to scale as they are solely intended to emphasise the points in the text.

There are not many sports apart from shooting where it is a distinct advantage to be a veteran.

Important Notes on Safety

The firer, coach and anyone associated with firearms must observe and maintain the relevant safety rules at all times on and off the range, and must never presume that a weapon is unloaded or that safety devices are applied or that the safety devices actually work.

Safety notes, as guidelines, are contained in each relevant chapter and you are advised to read through the book and familiarise themselves with each one, before handling firearms and commencing firing.

It is especially important that you fully understand the manufacturer's safety procedures as applicable to your particular firearms and accessories.

Neither the author or the publishers accept any responsibility of any kind from the use of this book and its contents even if advised of the possibility of any errors.

Handgun Development

Man has, by his nature, always sought to gain an edge over his opponents using various type of weapons over the years. This eventually led to the development of the matchlock, wheel-lock, flintlock and caplock firearms; each more reliable and accurate than the previous. This will to win is still as strong today in competitive shooting as it was when handguns were used for self defence.

The original handgun was a single shot weapon derived from the Horse Pistol; these were normally carried in pairs in holsters across the pommel of a saddle. Handguns have progressed over the years into highly accurate, high capacity and reliable weapons. This chapter highlights the main features of the development of the handgun.

Duelling Pistol

The grip was designed to allow the firer to point the pistol naturally at the target when coming up into the aim. The sights normally consisted of a bead foresight and a vee notch rear sight. By holding the handgun at arms length, consistent eye relief (the distance between the eye and the rear sight) is achieved. This ensured that the sight picture (the apparent size of the bead in relation to the notch) was correct each time the pistol was aimed.

It was also advisable to hold the handgun at arm's length to protect the eyes from fragments of flint, caps and burnt powder that could have been blown back. The percussion cap provided better reliability than the flash in the pan of the flintlock. Lock time was reduced and so were the incidents of hang fire as the firer was no longer concerned with keeping his powder dry in the pan.

Percussion Cap Duelling Pistol

Combat Revolver

Colt produced the first practical revolvers during the 1830's. The grip design assisted pointability and allowed the revolver to roll back in the hand, minimising the felt recoil and positioning the thumb so that the hammer could be cocked quickly for subsequent shots.

Allowing the muzzle to rise also assisted in displacing the fired percussion caps which otherwise might have caused a jam by falling between the hammer and the rear of the frame.

The vee notch rear sight and bead foresight, remained basically similar to previous handguns, although later models had a blade foresight.

1861 Colt Single Action Navy Revolver (Black Powder)

The notch, cut into the top of the hammer, resulted in the sight picture being lost when the hammer fell.

Colt (Sight Picture)

Any movement during the long throw of the hammer displaced the shot.

Authentic 1862 Colt Pocket Navy and Police Black Powder Revolvers with Uberti stainless steel replica above, also in .36 Calibre

Adams Solid Frame Double Action Revolver

This design of the 1850's enabled the hammer to be cocked by squeezing the trigger. The grip design prevented the hand from shifting during the long trigger pull and ensured that the position of the web between the thumb and trigger finger was consistent on the tang each time the weapon was drawn from the holster.

Adams Double Action Revolver
(Note the absence of a Hammer Spur)

Colt Side Hammer Revolver

Colt also used a solid frame on his side hammer revolver of 1855.

Colt Root Side Hammer Revolver

Smith & Wesson Model 1857

On the expiry of Colt's patent for a revolving cylinder, Smith & Wesson produced the first .22 rimfire cartridge revolver. They had previously obtained patent rights for a bored through cylinder which Colt had turned down.

Tip Up Revolver (Note Sheathed Trigger)

Smith & Wesson Tip Up Revolver

As the patent only applied in America, revolvers of this type were produced in the UK without the manufacturer's name or any serial number. The author's model has a brass frame and a 7 shot cylinder and is believed to have been made by Webley. To reload, the cylinder is taken out and the cases are ejected with the rod below the barrel. After loading the chambers the cylinder is then replaced.

Remington

In 1858 Remington also strengthened the design of their cap and ball revolver by making it a solid frame. A groove milled into the top strap acted as a rear sight and the foresight was fitted into a dovetail to provide lateral adjustment by drifting or by fitting a higher or lower sight for elevation. This model was also available with a fixed foresight.

Remington Single Action Revolver

Star

Star produced a trigger cocking model during the American Civil War which raised the hammer to enable it to be fired single action. The rear sight notch in the hammer was visible at full cock, which was similar to the Colt.

Reloading was speeded up by the top opening design and by replacing the cylinder with a pre-charged one. As single action thumb cocking remained the most popular for accurate shooting at this time, Star also manufactured a single action model, which reduced the trigger reach and pull (trigger pressure).

Top Opening Revolver

With the continued development of metallic cartridges in 1870, Smith & Wesson produced their top opening revolver. Empty cases were ejected as the revolver was opened, allowing a complete reload to be carried out quickly.

Smith & Wesson Top Opening Revolver .44 Rimfire

This revolver was single action with a foresight blade and a rear sight notch above the opening latch. Through custom and practise they were fired one handed at arms length. Smith & Wesson top opening revolvers were used at Wimbledon from 1885 to 1890, prior to the NRA moving to Bisley.

Merlin and Hulbert Revolver

Merlin and Hulbert were distributors for a number of manufacturers in addition to having handguns manufactured to their own designs. Revolvers produced without a licence for a bored through cylinder were sold as having been manufactured for Smith & Wesson

Merlin and Hulbert Revolver

This revolver was opened by rotating the barrel out of the dovetailed joints in its frame, located below the rear sight and cylinder pin; with the cases being ejected by pulling the barrel and cylinder forward.

Colt Front Loading Metallic Cartridge Revolver

As Smith & Wesson held the patent rights for a bored through cylinder, Colt converted a limited number of his Cap and Ball revolvers to a front loading tapered cartridge design by Thuer. Spent cases were ejected out of the front of each chamber in turn by cocking the revolver and aligning the extractor in front of the recoil shield with the chamber that had previously been fired and then dry firing off the action. The extractor pin was offset diagonally to the side of the chamber that was in line with the bore.

.38 Colt Front Loading Metallic Cartridge Revolver (note rear sight)

The 1861 model was converted in 1869 to fire rimless tapered central fire cartridges. In theory, fitting a rear sight in front of the forcing cone of the barrel should have improved the accuracy as the sights are fixed on to the solid barrel, rather than the rear sight notch being cut into the top of the hammer nose. In reality the resultant shorter sight base increased the angle of error in shot placement if the sights were mis-aligned.

Colt 'Cloverleaf' Model of 1871

On the expiry of White's patent for a bored through cylinder in 1869; which Smith & Wesson had secured, Colt produced a solid frame revolver with a 4 shot cylinder to fire low velocity .41 rimfire Deringer ammunition.

Colt Open Top Revolver

Colt also produced a 7 shot .22 revolver in 1871. A groove in the side of the frame enabled cartridges to be loaded and spent cartridges to be ejected without removing the cylinder. To unload, the ejector rod, in its housing on the lower right hand side of the barrel, is pushed to the rear after first aligning each chamber in turn with the groove.

Colt Open Top Revolver with Bird's Head Grip

Colt .44 Rimfire Model 1872

A loading gate was fitted into the frame to permit single ejection of empty cases and for reloading. It was similar in appearance to his Cap and Ball Army Model without the loading lever. The barrel length of the revolver illustrated has been shortened after leaving the factory; where they were produced with a 7.5" or 8" barrel.

Colt Single Action Revolver 1872

The sight picture was lost as the hammer fell, as was the case with Colt's cap and ball black powder revolvers. However, this had little effect on the practical accuracy.

Colt Model 1873

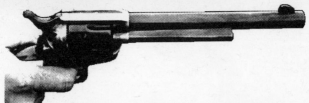

Colt Single Action Model 1873 with Ivory Grip

This model was manufactured with a solid frame, with a grooved rear sight and blade foresight. The sight picture is lost as the hammer falls.

Grooved Rear Sight

Blade Foresight

The hard rubber chequered grip, incorporating the Colt logo and later the American Eagle, offered a better hold than the smooth wood or ivory grips.

Target Shooting

As target practise evolved into the 'sport' of target shooting, manufacturers followed the lead of custom gunsmiths and produced handguns specifically designed for the sport.

Colt Flat Top Revolver

Colt Flat Top Model with Longer Grip produced from 1888

Changeable Foresight and Drift Adjustable Rear Sight

By raising the height of the sights the picture was not obscured behind the hammer spur as it fell.

Target Practise

At this time target shooting was considered a leisurely pursuit with the firer being allowed time to prepare for firing, which was a legacy from the cap and ball era.

To perfect the grip, the handgun was held in the non-firing hand whilst the correct grip was obtained with the strong hand. The weak hand then pushed it back into the firing hand to ensure that the grip was firm enough to stop the handgun from shifting in the hand during recoil.

Using reduced target loads for practise could result in a false sense of accuracy and security for police and service personnel, etc.

Colt Bisley 1894

The Bisley model modifications included re-contouring the grip to enable the hand to sit higher, in relation to the bore line. Lowering the hammer spur allowed it to be thumb cocked, without shifting the position of the hand. This also permitted the sight picture to be seen as the hammer fell. Shortening the hammer throw and reducing the strength of the main spring reduced the lock time and trigger pull. Also, a wider trigger increased the area over which to apply trigger pressure thus reducing the apparent pull.

Colt Bisley Revolver 1894

This model has fixed sights to comply with the match conditions.

Safety

Fitting a trigger shoe on a standard handgun can make the trigger wider than the trigger guard. This is potentially dangerous as the trigger is exposed on the outside of the guard and may be snagged on some object causing the gun to fire. A competitor in a practical pistol match shot himself in the foot. He was wearing a behind the hip holster at the time; the entry wound was in his buttock.

Winchester Revolver

A number of prototype revolvers were developed at the Winchester factory between 1875 and 1885 which included a 'swing out' cylinder design. None were produced commercially as agreements had been made with Smith & Wesson and Colt.

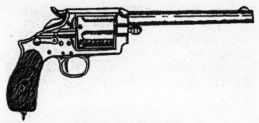

Winchester Revolver

Colt Double Action Revolvers

The Lightning, Thunderer and Frontier Models used the same method of unloading and reloading as the single action army model. The sight remained basically the same, with zeroing adjustments being made by bending the front sight or by turning the screw threaded barrel in a vice and by filing the sight to the required height.

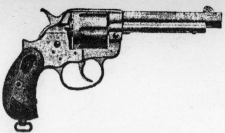

Colt 1878 Frontier Revolver

Fosbery Automatic Revolver 1900

This was a unique design, in that when fired, the cylinder and upper frame moved back with the recoil, automatically rotating the cylinder to align the next chamber with the bore. It was available in .455 calibre with a 6 shot cylinder and in .38 with a 7 shot cylinder.

Fosbery Automatic Revolver (Top opening)

Although the bore line is high in relation to the grip, recoil was manageable as it was absorbed by the working parts moving to the rear. The revolver was first fired at Bisley in 1900 and proved to be highly accurate and fast handling. This may be attributed to its shortened single action trigger pull and the tight manufacturing tolerances.

Improvements in the design of semi-automatic pistol ammunition made the pistol more reliable in adverse conditions, such as dust and mud etc; this therefore stopped the automatic revolver from becoming more popular.

Swing Out Cylinder Revolvers

By 1900 revolvers had evolved into the swing out cylinder models using a solid frame. These became the standard revolvers of the military and police.

The grip was designed to prevent the cases from snagging during unloading, when the ejector rod was pushed back.

Colt Swing Out Cylinder Revolver

Grip Fillers

With the re-design of the front and back strap, grip fillers were fitted to improve handling characteristics, particularly when using high velocity ammunition, and to obtain a consistent grip. These were available in small, medium and large sizes to fit the firer's hand.

Colt showing position of grip filler fitted

Target Models

These are fitted with wider sights, trigger, hammer spur and grips. A full length ejector shroud improves the balance and reduces recoil by increasing the mass.

Colt Revolver

The ventilated barrel rib as shown in the above picture, is to allow the heat to quickly dissipate so as to avoid distorting the sight picture through the effect of mirage.

Smith & Wesson Revolver

Ported Barrels

Barrels have also been ported to reduce recoil. The reduction in recoil enables the firer to quickly recover his sight picture ready for his next shot. Holes are preferably made by Spark Erosion and not simply by drilling, as Spark Erosion does not alter the hardening of the metal or leave rough tool marks. Stephen Alsop of S&S Systems designed one of the first UK Spark Erosion electronic machines in 1973 for this purpose.

Ported Barrel

Customised Revolver

The 'slab' sided barrel and weight have been left in the 'white' until the firer, who is having the gun customised (built) to his own specification, is satisfied that the amount of metal that has been removed has improved the balance before it is blued.

Customised Revolver based on a Smith & Wesson Model 10

Highly customised handguns have been built by gunsmiths to individual requirements and may be fitted with grips incorporating finger grooves, palm swell, palm shelf, thumb rest and tang.

Customised Grip

Semi Automatic Pistols

With the improvement and standardisation of ammunition, it became possible to produce reliable semi-automatic pistols at relatively low production costs when compared to earlier models, such as the Borchardt, Luger and Mauser pistols.

Colt 45 1911 ACP (Automatic Colt Pistol)

This was designed by John Browning and was the choice of the US army, as it offered increased firepower and speed of reloading when compared to the revolver.

The basic design of the combat handgun has changed little since the turn of the century, although improvements have been made in their reliability, handling characteristics, accuracy and materials used in construction.

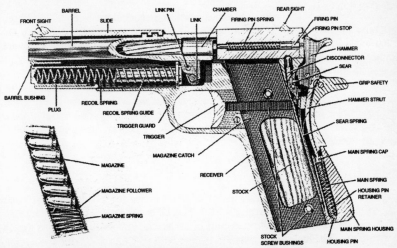

Colt Sectional View Showing Component Parts

Whilst being highly regarded as a 'man stopper' for combat use, it gained a poor reputation for accuracy. This was due mainly to the small foresight blade and rear sight notch, and the apprehension of the firer anticipating the recoil, particularly when being trained to fire it one handed.

The 1911 A1 model had the straight mainspring housing replaced with an arched one to improve natural pointing. The length of the grip safety tang was increased to stop the rear of the hammer spur from biting the web of flesh between the thumb and fore-finger, commonly called 'hammer bite'. The length of the trigger was shortened to reduce the reach. The frame was also relieved for the second pad of the trigger finger, so as to allow the finger to lie naturally on the trigger and to minimise the contact with the side of the frame. A Colt Gold Cup pistol is a modified 1911 A1 pistol, suitable for target shooting.

Colt 1911 A1 Pistol (Colt Gold Cup)

A customised Colt Gold Cup pistol is illustrated. Note the ambidextrous Safety Catch. Finger grooves in the front strap are formed by inserting half round strips of rubber under the wrap-around Packmayr rubber grips.

When Smith & Wesson produced their .35 semi-automatic pistol in 1913, they placed the grip safety in front of the fore strap at the right hand side. They also developed a bullet for the pistol, in which the jacketed head did not come into contact with the bore, due to it not extending past the shoulder of the 'round'. This improved the accuracy as the lead core of the bullet could take up the lands and grooves of the rifling better than a full metal jacketed bullet. It was also claimed that barrel wear was considerably reduced, by up to 95%.

Browning

Browning's improvements to his 1911 design led to the production in Belgium of his 9 mm High Power model of 1935 - designated HIGH POWER because of its 13 round magazine capacity to increase firepower and not because of any increase in stopping power over the .45 ACP (Automatic Colt Pistol).

Browning 9 mm High Power Pistol (Canadian)

The grip safety of the Colt, which was a requirement of the US Government, was not incorporated into the new design and the sights remained basically the same as the Colt's. During the Second World War manufacture of the pistol started in Canada.

The Canadian Browning had a serrated tapered foresight, commonly called a Barley Corn Sight, which arguably presented a better sight picture than those of the original Belgian model.

Sight Pictures

Belgium model

Canadian model

Colt and Browning now produce pistols based on their original designs as do a number of other manufacturers. These are used extensively in competition shooting.

SIG

SIG improved the accuracy of their service pistol by extending the length of the guide rails between the frame and slide and reducing the manufacturing tolerances for a tighter lockup.

Despite its inherent accuracy, the pistol's handling characteristics were generally considered less user-friendly than those of the Colt and Browning for action shooting. The magazine release is on the heel of the butt and not frame mounted at the rear of the trigger guard. The safety lever is positioned on the frame above where the magazine release is generally expected to be.

SIG 9 mm Pistol Target Model

This model is fitted with an adjustable rear sight and a longer barrel to extend the sight base.

Colt, Smith & Wesson and SIG Hammerli

These companies previously manufactured pistols to fire rimmed revolver ammunition and were highly accurate 'out of the box' handguns, specifically designed for target shooting in matches where a lower power floor than 9 mm Luger is permitted.

Colt .38 Mid Range Wadcutter

Smith & Wesson Model 52 .38 Mid Range Wadcutter

SIG Hammerli .38 Mid Range Wadcutter

Self Loading pistols are generally designed to fire round nosed jacketed rimless ammunition, which was originally designed by Browning. In order for a standard pistol to reliably feed semi wadcutter ammunition, the throat of the barrel and the feed ramp of a standard pistol would probably need to be polished.

Coonan .357 Magnum Combat Pistol

Coonan .357 Magnum Combat Pistol

Coonan produce a pistol in .357 Magnum which is generally considered to be revolver ammunition. By replacing the recoil spring with a weaker one, the lower power .38 Special ammunition may be used.

The Coonan is similar in design to the previously illustrated single action pistols.

Single Action

Single action pistols require that the first round is fed manually by drawing back the slide to the extent of its travel and releasing it. This feeds the round into the chamber and leaves the hammer cocked ready to fire.

Safety

When considering slowly lowering the hammer, by squeezing the trigger, when a round is in the chamber, a slip of the thumb can have serious consequences as the round will be fired.

Handgun Development

It was in this condition, hammer down with a round in the chamber, that the Colt .45 was holstered at the time when first issued as a service pistol to the US Army. It was later considered to be safer to stop this practise and to only holster the pistol with a loaded magazine, without a round in the chamber. When required to 'make ready', the slide was racked back and released to feed a round into the chamber and to cock the hammer. It is also faster to bring the pistol into action by racking back the slide, rather than thumb cocking, because the grip does not have to be altered as is the case when thumb cocking. This can be confirmed during dry firing practise.

Smith & Wesson Model 52 showing Slide held open (Racked Back)

Each time the weapon is fired the slide moves back as shown above. The slide cocks the hammer and on return feeds the next round into the chamber.

Double Action

A double action pistol is one where the hammer can be cocked by a long pull on the trigger, which raises and then releases the hammer.

Walther P38

Walther P38 Pistol

This pistol is generally considered to be the first double action combat pistol that was available in substantial numbers. The design permitted the first shot to be fired by a long pull on the trigger, which raised and then released the hammer to fire the first round (which had previously been fed into the chamber and the hammer lowered). The hammer was cocked for the second and subsequent shots by the rearward movement of the slide after each shot.

Handgun Development

Neither the long trigger pull nor thumb cocking is considered suitable for competition shooting and is discouraged by match conditions, for example, in Service Pistol A and PP2 you are not allowed to carry a pistol in a holster with a round in the chamber.

Some double action pistols of modern design enable the hammer to be lowered safely onto a loaded chamber, for example, the SIG Sauer with a de-cocking lever.

Safety

The manufacturer's safety literature regarding a particular handgun should be read and complied with before commencing weapon handling.

Springfield Armory P9 Pistol

This particular model may be carried cocked with the safety catch applied (cocked & locked) or with the hammer down and the safety catch applied.

Single and Double Action Trigger Reach

Smith & Wesson .45 Pistol

This Smith & Wesson pistol was designed for practical pistol shooting where single action shooting is preferred. Note the shorter trigger reach and the hang of the trigger in comparison with the double action mode as shown on the P9 pistol above.

Selecting a Handgun

There is a wide choice of handguns to suit different preferences, shooting styles and shooting disciplines.

Selecting a Handgun

The first choice of an individual entering into the sport is usually dictated by a personal preference for a revolver or pistol which may have been previously owned. A gun being previously owned may indicate that the last owner was not entirely satisfied with the handgun or it may be that he is trading up to a more accurate and reliable handgun. The choice of a pistol or revolver is also usually influenced by a particular discipline.

Ruger modern Cap and Ball Revolver

Rogers and Spencer Revolver with Adjustable Sights

Customised Double Action Revolver

Ruger Single Action Revolver

Smith & Wesson Pistol

Selecting a Handgun

SIG Sauer Pistol

Colt Gold Cup Pistol

Note the undercut target foresight on the Colt Gold Cup pistol.

Before deciding to purchase a handgun, it is essential to consider the criteria that it will have to meet.

Reliability

The handgun must be reliable as no time is allowed for malfunctions in action shooting events.

Handling Characteristics

Handling characteristics can be confirmed by being able to manipulate the controls with one hand without altering your grip of the gun. The handgun must point naturally at the target. (This can only be achieved if the firer's position is correctly aligned with the target).

Accuracy

After confirming accuracy by bench resting, apply the essentials of good shooting again from a comfortable unsupported stance. Aiming for the potential accuracy, the grouping standard achieved will give an indication of the practical accuracy of the gun in the hand of the firer at this stage in his training (the coach may also demonstrate the accuracy by firing the gun).

A standard handgun of modern manufacture is capable of producing a 50 mm group at 10m providing the essentials of good marksmanship have been mastered. Until this is achieved few points will be gained by 'trading up' the handgun against the cost of practising. The firer should not progress to firing from longer ranges until this 50 mm standard is achieved.

The firer, after reaching his potential accuracy at longer ranges, for example, a 150 mm group at 25m, may consider employing a gunsmith to work on the handgun to improve its accuracy and handling characteristics, in order to improve his scores.

Service pistols are designed for reliability in adverse conditions, for example, dust, mud, etc. The manufacturing tolerances are therefore deliberately not as tight as those found on a target pistol. There are exceptions to this, for example, the SIG.

In practical terms, a service handgun using hard ball (round nosed jacketed) ammunition cannot be expected, in the hands of an individual who has just entered into handgun shooting or who has received little or no coaching, to group as tightly as a target pistol or revolver, when using reduced target loads. For example, .38 mid range wadcutter.

Accuracy is not only dependent on the application of the firer's chosen marksmanship techniques. The firer must be **confident** that his handgun is reliable as any doubt will not allow him to concentrate on the essentials of good shooting.

Sights

Sights have a significant effect on the potential accuracy of the handgun. On a service handgun, the sights, as issued, are normally of snag-free design. With this type of sight, the 'blueing' can become worn through holster wear. This then allows the sight to reflect light making it difficult to focus on the tip of the foresight, resulting in a blurred sight picture.

Various sights have been designed to improve the sight picture, for example, 3 dot, coloured insert, white outline etc.

Iron Sights (White Outline)

It is generally accepted that these are more suitable for low light conditions and that a black undercut, non reflective sight picture is preferred for target shooting rather than the ramped foresight as illustrated.

Misfires and Stoppages

A misfire can be attributed to:

1. **Ammunition Related:**
   a) Faulty primer.
   b) No powder loaded in the case. (In this event, a muffled report will be heard). No attempt should be made to fire a further shot until the barrel has been checked to ensure it is clear of an obstruction as the power of the primer is sufficient to drive the bullet into the barrel, possibly lodging it there. This can result in a burst barrel if a subsequent shot is fired.

2. **Handgun Related:**
   a) Light hammer throw (weak mainspring).
   b) Hammer binding on the side of the recess.
   c) Mechanical defect in the gun.

Stoppages (Jams) can be attributed to:

1. **Primer not seated correctly in the case.**
   If protruding against the face of the recoil shield this can prevent the cylinder turning. It is also very dangerous as the primer may be crushed, resulting in a chamber being discharged before the cylinder is fully closed.

2. **Misfeeding.**
   This may be caused by damaged magazine lips, angle of feed ramp or a weak slide return spring. To reduce the possibility of misfeeding, after racking back the slide it should be released quickly and not eased forward slowly.

3. **Hard extraction.**
   This may be caused by excessive pressure expanding the case against the chamber walls, or it may be attributed to firing longer cases, for example, .357 magnum in chambers that have been previously 'fouled' when using shorter .38 cases.

4. **Worn or build-up of fouling behind the extractor.**
   This prevents the extractor taking hold on the rim of the cartridge case.

5. **Damaged Ejector.**
   This will stop ejection of the case.

6. **Slide not travelling back sufficiently.**
   If the slide does not travel back far enough to enable the base of the spent case to be struck by the ejector, the case will jam. This problem can be caused by using down-loaded ammunition or the power of the return spring being too strong.

7. **Holding the pistol loosely.**
   This may take out the inertia of the slide travelling back to eject the fired case. This can also produce a stoppage with a Webley Fosbery revolver.

8. Using soft lead bullets.

This can result in the nose of the round 'biting' into the mouth of the chamber throat as it is forced from the magazine's lips up the feed ramp.

Revolver Modifications

Modifications are undertaken to improve the handling, reliability and accuracy characteristics of a handgun. They should only be undertaken by a competent gunsmith. The following is an example of a customised match revolver.

Davis National Match Revolver, 1 of 500

Handling

This is improved by:

1. Fitting replacement grips.

A covered or open backstrap will lengthen or shorten the trigger reach. Grips incorporating a grip filler, finger grooves, palm swell, thumb rest and tang may be custom made to the individual's hand size.

2. The balance can be altered by fitting a barrel weight .

This also minimises the initial movement caused by pulse or muscle tremors and reduces muzzle rise during recoil.

3. Porting the barrel to reduce muzzle rise.

This allows the gases to escape in an upward direction, reducing the pressure at the muzzle end, before the bullet leaves the barrel.

4. Chamfering the chamber mouth assists in reloading.

5. Fitting an enlarged thumb cylinder release latch.

When fitted to a Smith & Wesson it avoids having to shift the grip during reloading with the left hand.

Reliability

This is improved by:

1. **Timing adjustment.**
   Misalignment between chambers and bore will result in lead being shaved off the bullet, resulting in erratic shooting. There may be a minimal amount of play on the cylinder when the trigger and hammer are at rest. There must be no significant lateral or radial movement of the cylinder when the trigger is held to the rear and the hammer is falling. Cylinder end-float should be reduced to the practical minimum for uniform ignition of the primer.

2. **Correct Hammer Throw.**
   A Light hammer throw will cause misfires due to an insufficient strike on the primer. Service ammunition requires a heavy blow as do certain makes of primers which are used when hand loading the ammunition.

Accuracy

This is improved by the following:

1. **Fit adjustable target or optical sights,**
   to enable a precise zero and a clearer sight picture to be obtained.

2. **Fit a match bull barrel with rifling twist,**
   to suit the burning rate of the powder and bullet weight of the ammunition being used.

3. **Polish the trigger notch and sear.**
   to reduce the trigger pull.

4. **Fit a trigger stop,**
   to eliminate over travel which can result in pulling the shot low.

5. **Port the barrel**
   to reduce recoil and muzzle flip to speed up sight alignment ready for subsequent shots.

Pistol Modifications

Modifications are undertaken to improve the handling, reliability and accuracy characteristics of a handgun. They should only be undertaken by a competent gunsmith. The following are two examples of modified pistols.

Customised Pistols

Handling

This is improved by the following:

1. **Lengthen or shorten the trigger reach.**
   This can be achieved on the Colt pistol by replacing the mainspring housing with an arched, semi-arched or flat housing, or by replacing the trigger with a longer or shorter one. Replace the grips with thicker or thinner stocks.

2. **Checker parts of the gun.**
   Checker the front and rear strap of the grip frame and the front and the underside of the trigger guard to obtain a secure grip.

3. **Lower the bore line.**
   The underside of the trigger guard, where it meets the frame, may be relieved to allow the second finger of the firing hand to sit higher; this enables the bore line to be lowered in relation to the hand.

4. **Fit extended controls to improve handling characteristics.**
   The safety catch, slide release and magazine release may be extended to improve ease of use.

5. **Modify the magazines.**
   Bevelling the magazine well and fitting a magazine chute and buffer pad to the base of the magazines speeds reloading.

6. **Modify the slide.**
   Serrate the front of the slide for an easier grip or fit a cocking handle to rack back the slide when a thumb guard or an optical sight is fitted.

7. **Fit an enlarged grip safety,**
   to spread the kick of the recoil over a wider area of the hand.

Reliability

This is improved by the following:

1. **Ensure the magazine does not misfeed.**
   If a magazine misfeeds, renew it or use it for practise only.

2. **Polish the feed ramp and throat barrel,**
   to assist feeding;

3. **Replace springs.**
   Replace the recoil, mainspring and firing pin springs.

4. **Check the Safety devices.**
   Check the half cock notch, safety catch, grip safety, magazine safety, hammer firing pin block, de-cocking lever, etc. Have any been disconnected?

Accuracy

This is improved by the following:

1. **Fit adjustable target or optical sights,**
   to enable a precise zero and a clearer sight picture to be obtained.

2. **Fit a match bull barrel with rifling twist**
   to match the ammunition being used.

3. **Polish the trigger notch and sear**
   to obtain a smooth release of the hammer.

4. **Fit a trigger stop,**
   to eliminate over travel which can result in pulling the shot low.

5. **Fit a compensator,**
   to reduce recoil and to speed up sight alignment ready for subsequent shots. It may also extend the sight base.

6. **Fit a recoil buffer,**
   to cushion the metal to metal contact as the slide moves back.

7. **Reduce the fitting tolerances of the slide to frame and replace the barrel bushing,**
   to improve lockup.

Handgun Modifications

Over chamfering the chambers on a revolver can increase the head space, which is the distance between the base of the case and the recoil shield, or it can leave the case unsupported. Either can result in a ruptured case.

Over polishing the throat of the barrel in a pistol can also leave the case unsupported, resulting in a breech explosion.

Fitting a new barrel in a pistol may also affect the lockup and head spacing if not gauged correctly.

Fitting a trigger bearing stop to the rear of the trigger guard offers a smooth release of the shot and prevents over travel.

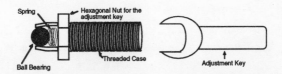

Trigger Bearing Stop

A trigger stop fitted onto a revolver to prevent over travel, can affect the timing (alignment of chambers and bore) if fitted incorrectly. Epoxying a piece of rubber onto the rear of the trigger or the guard, in order to stage the trigger, is dangerous. This is usually done in an attempt to hold the hammer back whilst concentrating on the sight picture, then compressing the rubber to allow the hammer to fall. This does not offer a smooth release of the shot as there is an interruption in squeezing through the trigger. Also, as the rubber becomes worn or loses its elasticity, the shot may then become a negligent discharge.

A trigger job will give a smooth release of the hammer, minimising any disturbance to the sight picture during the initial movement, providing that the new notch (bent) does not shear because too much metal has been removed or it has not been re-hardened.

With the increase in the use of compensators, optical sights and large capacity magazines, gunsmiths and manufacturers have lightened the slides by removing surplus metal from 'non-critical areas' to speed up the slide in its travel and to improve the balance and handling characteristics.

It is advisable to have a competent gunsmith carry out the work

Reducing Recoil

The use of aluminium and polymer frames has led to an increase in recoil because of the guns being of less mass. Recoil can be reduced by having the barrel compensated and/or by fitting a recoil buffer. The buffer replaces the return spring guide rod and cushions the effect of recoil on the handgun and firer. As the recovery time is reduced, accuracy is improved because the sights are re-aligned more quickly.

Fitting Replacement Sights

Low profile sights that are milled into the slide are generally preferred as they are closer to the bore line and can be aligned quickly, when pointing naturally.

There is a tendency with sights that are mounted high above the bore line, for the firer to point naturally when coming up into the aim and then having to lower the handgun to align the sights with the aiming mark, thus losing valuable time.

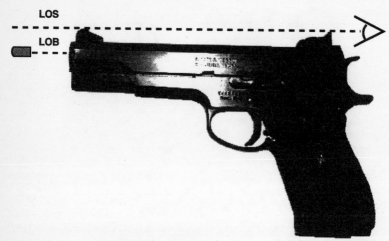

Line of Sight in relation to Line of Bore

Note the trigger stop and undercut foresight.

High sights will also increase the effect of canting. High visibility combat sights do not refer to the height above the bore line, only that they are wide enough to see quickly for practical shooting.

Gun Handling & Equipment

Weapon handling should be practised with an unloaded gun until it becomes instinctive. This is achieved by thinking every action through. As the firer becomes confident in his handling skills, his scores will improve because he is able to concentrate on his shooting techniques rather than being concerned with his actions.

Dry Firing

Dry Firing practise should be carried out with snap caps in place, ideally with inert spring-loaded primers to absorb the blow to the firing pin and to cushion the blow of the hammer on the rear of the frame or slide. If a 9 mm Browning (Model 35) is dry fired without snap caps, the firing pin retaining plate may fracture, releasing the firing pin back towards the firer when live firing, possibly resulting in an injury.

Dry firing is invaluable as it allows weapon handling, trigger control, loading and unloading to be practised at any time in the privacy of your own home. It should not be practised on the range without the permission of the Range Conducting Officer, (RCO), and then only in designated areas, such as on the firing point.

When considering using empty cases to dry fire, ensure that they have been fire formed in the chamber of the same handgun. The author once had the unpleasant experience of having to push a brass dowel rod down a barrel to force back the working parts (the case had previously been fired in an SMG). This resulted in breaking the firing pin which went unnoticed until the handgun was required to be fired.

Dry Grouping Practise

Correct sight alignment can be confirmed by setting up the handgun in a suitable rest at eye level. The firer, standing an arms length away from the gun so as to ensure that the eye relief is correct, aligns the sights with the centre of the aiming mark or disc, which is moved over a plain target by the coach on the instructions of the firer (for example, up, down, left and right), until the firer is satisfied that he has obtained the correct point of aim, (POA).

The coach, when informed by the firer that he has the correct point of aim, marks the backing target with a pin hole before moving the disc away from the LOS. The size of the pin hole group can then be ascertained using this dry grouping practise.

Any spread in the group is due entirely to variations in the firer's sight alignment, as the gun is held firmly in the rest and therefore the spread cannot be attributed to variations in the firer's grip, etc.

Aiming Disc

Aiming Disc

A large white map pin held against a dark backing paper, 3m from the gun muzzle, provides a suitable aiming disc.

A 1 mm error in sight alignment at 3m will displace a subsequent pin hole by 20 mm if the gun has a 150 mm sight base.

A 10 mm group of pinholes at 3m in theory would equate to a 50 mm group at 15m (the group spreads by a factor of five due to the range increasing by a factor of five).

Range Safety Rules

These state that during the load, unload and when clearing stoppages, the weapon must point down the range in the direction of the target.

Safety - before reading further see: Range Danger Area and Quadrant Elevation.

Loading a Revolver

On being given the order to load a revolver, it should only be tilted forward to assist in 'charging' the chambers. The barrel should then be brought up horizontal before closing the cylinder to 'load.'

Unloading a Revolver

To fully unload; open the cylinder before raising the muzzle in order to eject the brass, misfires, etc from the chambers. This prevents cases from being snagged by the grip panel, (as shown in the illustration) and possibly resulting in the star of the extractor overriding the rim of the case, leaving it in the chamber.

Unloading a Colt Single Action or S&W Top Opening Revolver

When using a revolver with a loading gate or a top opening design, etc, the firer should first 'clear' any doubts with the Range Officer who may not be familiar with the handling characteristics of the particular weapon, which may require that the muzzle is lowered or raised to load or unload.

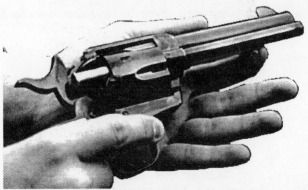

Unloading a Single Action Colt

Unsafe Conduct

A common occurrence when unloading, is the firer holding the handgun across the front of his body, thus pointing the barrel along the firing line!

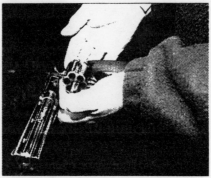

Unloading a Revolver Incorrectly

Unloading a Pistol Incorrectly. (Note the finger is also on the trigger)

How would you like to face this - even though it may be an empty threat?

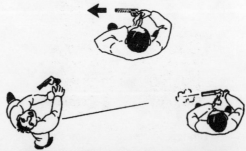

Incorrect Alignment when Unloading

The rules state that during the load, unload, making safe or any stoppage drills, the weapon must be pointing down range in the direction of the target.

To comply with the rule, the body should be turned oblique to the line of fire before unloading, so as to ensure that the weapon is always pointing down the range. This can be achieved by bending the knees to pivot the upper part of the body.

Correct Alignment when Unloading

Bend the knees and pivot to avoid moving the feet, as natural pointing at the target may be lost when returning to the position after reloading.

Revolver Speed Loading

In the earlier illustration, 'Loading a Revolver', the firer is shown to be charging the chambers with his weak hand using a speed loader pre-charged with 6 rounds. A technique which may be more natural for a right handed firer is to operate the cylinder latch to release the cylinder and then use the weak hand to swing out the cylinder to eject the cases, whilst the strong hand reaches for the speed loader to reload. The weak hand is then left to close the cylinder whilst the strong hand perfects the grip.

This technique avoids loading the cylinder at an unnatural angle which could result in 'fumbling' the load.

Speed Loaders

Speed Loading a Revolver

Security

The handgun and ammunition should not be left unattended on the range. After unloading and showing clear, the weapon should be holstered (hammer down, pistol magazine removed) before going forward to score and patch - after being informed by the RCO that the range is clear and that it is permissible to go forward.

Holsters

The type of holster is usually dictated by the discipline being fired. In the Army Rifle Association (ARA) match, the webbing holster, as issued, must be used for Service Pistol (SP). A good tip is to leave an empty magazine in the attached pouch or the cleaning rod in its internal pocket as this will assist in making the holster rigid.

Holsters suitable for the other disciplines are manufactured from leather, abrasion resistant nylon and plastic.

Safety

Suitable holsters usually exclude cross draw holsters or shoulder holsters as the handgun may sweep across the firing line during the draw.

Competition Rigs

These are the most popular as the belt, holster and pouch are held rigid, using metal or plastic inserts. The belt may also be restrained from movement by using the belt loops in the trousers or belt keeper. Velcro may also be attached to the trousers and belt.

The open front holster, worn in front of the hip, offers the fastest draw. The drop loop holds the handgun away from the body so as to present the firer with the correct grip.

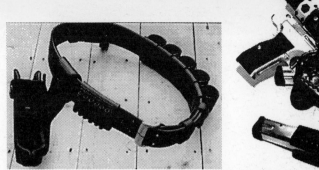

Open Front Holsters, Front and Side View

A behind the hip holster is designed to fit the handgun into the small of the back for concealment.

The match conditions may state that the trigger guard is covered and that any fitted retention devices must be applied.

Behind the Hip Holsters

Essentials of Marksmanship
(Handgun)

When drawing from the holster, ensure that the **grip is correct** and that the **stable position adopted** enables the handgun to **point naturally** at the target. On coming up into the aim, concentrate on the **sight picture** whilst **controlling breathing** and **squeeze the trigger to release the shot**.

- **Correct Grip**
- **Stable Position**
- **Point Naturally**
- **Sight Picture**
- **Control Breathing**
- **Squeeze Trigger**

Techniques

The techniques selected by the firer must be 'comfortable', 'co-ordinated' and 'give confidence'.

Shooting Practise

As shooting practise evolved into the sport of target shooting, firers modified the duelling stance to gain a comfortable, stable position, pointing naturally at the target, with the correct eye relief.

The stance which is adopted is dictated by the necessity to 'see' the sights clearly, (eye relief) as eye strain is uncomfortable and thus causes errors.

Duelling Stance

Oblique Stance

Open Stance

Note the change of eye relief with each stance.

Stance

The stance adopted by the firer is further dictated by his build. Consistency is achieved by the positioning of the feet, in relation to the line of fire (LOF).

Duelling Stance

This stance was originally used by duellists so as to offer the minimum target profile to an adversary. They sometimes lowered their forearm towards their chest into the line of fire, by bending the wrist and elbow, in an attempt to deflect the projectile away from the vital organs.

Grip

The strength of the grip is dictated by the control required to recover from the recoil for subsequent shots. Too firm a grip can make the hand begin to tremble and too weak a grip can allow the handgun to shift in the hand.

Imagine holding a drinks can - too hard a grip will crush the can and the contents will erupt, whereas too loose a grip will allow the can to slip through the hand.

When taking up the grip, apply pressure on the front strap with the two middle fingers, with the thumb and little finger resting on the grip. The trigger finger should lie naturally on the trigger.

Trigger Finger Placement

Ideally, the first joint of the trigger finger should rest against the side of the trigger to ensure that the finger is placed consistently each time the trigger is squeezed. The firer is often advised to use the centre of the first pad as it is considered to be the most sensitive part of the finger to feel the trigger pressure. This does not present a problem during deliberate shooting practices, for example, grouping and zeroing, with low powered ammunition. It will probably be found that during later rapid practises, particularly when using higher velocity ammunition, that the precise placement of the trigger finger is lost from shot to shot. It is therefore recommended to use the first joint in order to obtain consistency.

Trigger Finger Placement

Dry firing practise is required to co-ordinate the pressure required by the fingers. A trigger pull which is too light may result in too loose a grip and a trigger pull which is too heavy may result in a firm grip. The brain has to send conflicting information to the trigger finger and the two middle fingers at the same time, as well as concentrating on the sight picture and controlling breathing.

Essentials of Marksmanship

Imagine trying to squeeze off 2.5 lbs (1 Kg) of trigger pressure whilst maintaining too firm a grip with the two middle fingers.

This problem may be partially overcome by using a two handed grip.

Natural Pointing

The experienced firer always obtains natural pointing with the target/s as he adopts his position.

This is achieved by aligning the body position so that the handgun points naturally at the target. If the handgun does not point naturally at the target, your body will automatically try to adjust into a comfortable position, rather than strain, resulting in displacement of the shot.

Pointing naturally should be achieved without any undue physical effort. There is usually a tendency for the muscles to relax after releasing the shot, resulting in disturbing the 'lay' of the handgun whilst the bullet is still travelling down the barrel.

Natural Pointing

Testing and Adjusting

When given the opportunity to test and adjust onto your target/s, confirm pointability by aiming at the aiming mark, then lower the pistol. On coming back into the aim, the sight should be on or near the aiming mark. If not, move the position of the feet and re-confirm.

Care should be taken not to shorten or lengthen the eye relief. (The apparent size of the rear sight notch in relation to the foresight post).

Master Eye

Firers normally have one eye which is stronger than the other. To determine which is the master eye, look at the target, hold your arm outstretched and point your index finger at the target. Focus on the target, keeping both eyes open; an optical illusion occurs, enabling you to 'see' through your finger. Close each eye alternately. The eye which is aiming the finger at the target is the master eye, whereas the weak eye will be aiming off.

This optical illusion can be used to the firer's advantage when engaging targets quickly. By keeping both eyes open when coming up into the aim, the Point of Aim can still be seen through the hands and handgun, allowing natural pointing to be achieved by bending the knee/s.

Canting

The head must be upright with the pupil in the centre of the eye socket. Canting the head may result in squinting out of the corner of the eye, impeding vision.

Canted sight may not significantly affect the fall of shot; however, what will affect it is an inconsistent grip and position.

When firing with the weak hand, using the duelling stance, a technique used by a number of firers in an attempt to move the MPI or HPA onto the centre of the target is to cant the handgun by pivoting the wrist, in order to change the initial movements or jump of the gun.

The eye can detect errors in sight alignment faster when there is no horizontal error. No attempt should be made to aim off by raising or lowering the foresight above the top of the rear sight or permitting more light at either side of the post.

Sight Picture

The correct sight picture can only be obtained by ensuring that the tip of the foresight is level with the top of the rear sight when the post is central in its notch. This can only be achieved by focusing on the sights against a blurred target. It will be seen that the rear sight also appears to be slightly blurred as the focus is concentrated on the tip of the foresight.

Shooting glasses with prescription lenses enable the firer with poor eye sight to focus on the foresight tip at arm's length.

Correct Sight Picture

The distance of the target dictates how unfocused it will be. The example shows the correct sight picture on releasing the shot.

Blurred Sight Picture

Focusing on the target will result in a blurred sight picture, possibly resulting in a sight alignment error.

The apparent size of the rear sight notch in relation to the foresight post is vitally important. Fitting a wider foresight with a compatible rear sight notch to suit the individual firer's eye relief will improve the inherent accuracy of any handgun.

Aiming

This can never become instinctive although with practise it can be speeded up. Even the firer with poor eyesight needs only to concentrate on the tip of the foresight in the centre of the rear sight to improve his standard of shooting.

10 years ago the author suffered an eye injury caused by an ejected case. This resulted in his vision being impaired although it did not significantly effect his shooting, as he can still focus on the foresight tip which is only an arm's length away.

Aiming Errors

If both eyes are kept open, especially when trying to focus on the sight, the master eye illusion will occur, making it difficult to concentrate on the foresight tip, therefore it is advisable to close the weak eye.

Angular Errors in Sight Alignment

These are caused by not having the foresight tip and the top of the rear sight notch precisely aligned; this usually occurs when the firer is focusing on the target and not on the sights.

It is vitally important that the tip of the foresight is central in the rear sight notch. When coming up into the aim, focus on the aiming mark and align the unfocused sights in the centre of the mass (target) whilst taking up the first pressure on the trigger and controlling breathing. During the natural pause in breathing, concentrate on the foresight in the centre of the rear sight notch, which should now be aligned with the unfocused POA - and release the shot.

1 mm Rule

If the focus is on the aiming mark on the target at the moment of firing, the sights will be blurred and the sight alignment may not be correct. This will result in an angle of error.

For example; if the foresight tip is 1 mm higher and 1 mm off centre, with a sight base of 150 mm (the distance between the foresight and the rear sight) this will give a 1 mm angular error in sight alignment both vertically and laterally in the length of the sight base. Therefore, for every 150 mm in range there is a 1 mm displacement of the shot both vertically and laterally. This means that the shot will be displaced 100 mm (4 inches) vertically and laterally at a range of 15 metres.

The following fall of shot is the result of a 1 mm angular error in the sight base when firing at various ranges. The illustration shows the mean point of impact (MPI) at each range and not a shot within the mean group size caused by the random dispersal of the shots within a group.

Essentials of Marksmanship

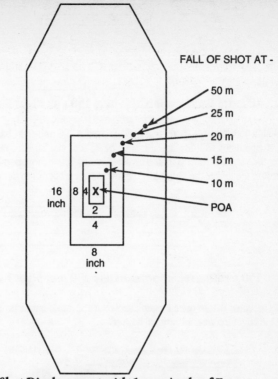

FALL OF SHOT AT -

50 m
25 m
20 m
15 m
10 m
POA

16 inch

8 4 X
2
4

8 inch

Shot Displacement with 1 mm Angle of Error

Note: the shots are not displaced in a straight, diagonal line due to the drift of the bullet caused by the rifling twist at longer ranges. For every 5m in range, the MPI will be displaced by approximately 33 mm as the following table shows:

Shot Displacement at various ranges with a 1 mm Angle of Error

Range in m	Range in mm	Sight Base		Displacement
10	10,000	÷ 150 mm	=	67 mm
15	15,000	÷ 150 mm	=	100 mm
20	20,000	÷ 150 mm	=	133 mm
25	25,000	÷ 150 mm	=	167 mm
50	50,000	÷ 150 mm	=	333 mm

Sight Base

Handguns with a 100 mm (4") barrel will typically have a 150 mm sight base and so a 1 mm error in sight alignment will displace the shot by 100 mm at 15m, as explained previously.

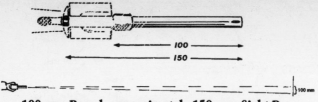

100 mm Barrel, approximately 150 mm Sight Base

Handguns with a 150 mm (6") barrel will typically have a 200 mm sight base and so a 1 mm error in sight alignment will displace the shot by 75 mm at 15m - a 25% improvement in accuracy over the same distance. 6" barrel revolvers are therefore more popular in competition shooting because the longer the sight base, the less the angle of error in sight alignment.

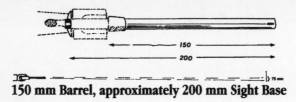

150 mm Barrel, approximately 200 mm Sight Base

It is generally accepted that to use a longer barrel than 150 mm is impractical, due to the speed of engaging the target from a conventional holster.

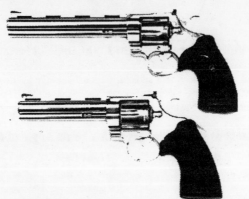

Colt Python Revolvers, 6" and 8" Barrels

The above Colt Python revolvers are fitted with Packmayr grips which are preferred by a number of firers to the standard ones as supplied 'out of the box'.

Focusing Errors

The further apart the rear sight and foresight become, the more difficult it is for the eye to focus on both at the same time. Even though the angular error is reduced, there comes a point at which it is more difficult to focus on both, so focusing errors are introduced. The ideal sight base for a pistol is equal to the depth of focus of the eye when looking at the sights an arm's length away. This appears to be approximately 175 mm for the average person.

Individual's Sight Base

The author once attempted to have a handgun custom built which he believed would improve the accuracy. Starting with a new Colt Gold Cup .45 pistol, which is a highly accurate 'out of the box' handgun, a 150 mm (6") match barrel was fitted with a barrel weight milled to the contours of the front of the slide and frame to dampen the effect of recoil on subsequent shots (similar to that on a Browning Competition model). An undercut foresight was fixed to the front of the barrel weight to extend the sight base by 30 mm (1.20"). The attempt failed because the author had extended the foresight beyond his depth of focus. Refitting the foresight in its original position confirmed his ideal sight base as the accuracy was returned.

Browning Competition Model

When using a revolver the author prefers the Colt Single Action with a 4.75" barrel. Ideally, a newcomer to the sport should try various club handguns with different barrel lengths and sights to confirm which offers him the best consistent sight picture.

Breathing Control

Failure to control breathing results in the shot going high or low, for example, breathing in, when aiming a pistol, causes the barrel to rise and breathing out causes it to fall. The normal breathing cycle takes approximately 4 seconds. There is a natural pause after breathing out before breathing in again.

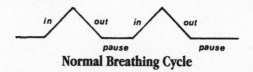

Normal Breathing Cycle

The natural pause between breathing can be extended for up to 6 seconds. Any longer results in straining in the aim, as the brain needs oxygen through the blood stream to enable the eye to concentrate on the sight picture.

The firer should breathe in deeply once, to oxygenate the body. On being asked, 'Are you ready'?, he should then take shallow breaths before the targets are exposed, releasing the shot/s during the pause when he has breathed out; breathing normally between exposures.

Breathing Cycle Showing Extended Pause

Shot Release

Trigger pressure is normally in two parts as a safety precaution.

The first part, taking up the slack, should be done as the arm is extended. The second part is to steadily increase the pressure during breathing out, so as to release the shot during the pause in breathing whilst concentrating on the correct sight picture.

Safety

The trigger pressure should be confirmed during dry firing practises because not all firearms have this first safety feature.

Snatching the trigger will pull the shot to the right (right handed firer). Suddenly releasing it will displace the shot to the left as the bullet is still travelling down the barrel.

After releasing the trigger, ensure that the trigger finger is re-positioned correctly for subsequent shots. To maintain consistency, squeeze directly to the rear, ensuring that the grip pressure being applied is the same from shot to shot. This can be practised dry using a double action pistol, or the firer can be assisted by the coach cocking the hammer back to fire single action, thus avoiding the firer having to alter his grip. When dry firing without the assistance of a coach, the firer should use the thumb of the supporting hand to cock the hammer to avoid altering the grip with his firing hand.

The coach may use a length of fishing line, or something similar, attached to the hammer, passed over the firer's shoulder to cock the action. This also simulates recoil which can be used to confirm the consistency of the firers' grip for subsequent dry shots and to practise recovery from recoil.

Essentials of Marksmanship

Consistent Grip

A consistent grip must be obtained for dry and live firing.

Combat Handgun Techniques

Modern combat handguns are designed to be fired using both hands, whenever possible.

Beretta Pistol (note re-curved front of trigger guard)

Adopting the Stance

The stance adopted by the firer is dictated by the position of the feet, modified to suit the firer's build, eye relief or when firing from cover.

Isosceles Stance

This is similar to the open duelling stance. The feet are parallel to the target and approximately 450 mm apart. The arms are outstretched with the elbows locked; this ensures that the eye relief is consistent for each shot and allows the arms and body weight to counteract recoil.

Natural pointing is achieved by moving the position of the feet or by bending the knee/s to align the upper body when engaging multiple targets quickly.

The stance takes its name from the triangular position.

Isosceles Stance

The stance offers stability, consistent eye relief and unrestricted breathing, whilst keeping the head upright, allowing a left or right master eye to be used. The disadvantage is that it is impractical to use when firing around cover.

Right Handed Firer with a Left Master Eye

Weaver Stance

This stance takes its name from an American police officer. The position of the feet are similar to when using a shoulder held weapon. The stance is oblique to the line of fire, with the firing arm outstretched to gain maximum eye relief. This ensures that the eye relief and sight picture remains consistent. By bending the elbow of the supporting arm and pulling back with the hand, the effect of recoil can be counteracted.

Weaver Stance

Care should also be taken not to cant the head as this can lead to impeding the vision, with the pupil not being central in the eye socket.

Firers of a large build may also experience restriction in breathing, due to the arm being locked

Essentials of Marksmanship

across the chest. They may modify the stance by raising the elbow of the supporting arm away from the body.

Cross Stance

This modified stance may be described as a 'cross stance' which is between an Isosceles and a Weaver stance.

The stance offers stability and speed of engagement. (High visibility combat sights are recommended to offset the loss of eye relief which occurs when using the Weaver Stance). This position is practical and may be used when engaging targets around cover and, when in competitions, within foot fault lines.

High Visibility Combat Sights

This type of design extends the sight base slightly thus reducing the effect of an angle of error in sight alignment.

FBI Stance

This developed from the Duellist stance. The non firing arm is held across the chest with the fist clenched, (similar to a Roman salute), to brace the upper body. This technique was optimistically used by the FBI to protect the vital organs with the forearm, when not wearing body armour.

Tactical Stance

A technique that may be adopted when firing around cover is to step up to the post or barricade with the firing side foot. Extend the arm out fully whilst bringing the body round, by bending the knees and moving the inside foot. This stance does not require the firer to cant the head or lean out from cover.

Tactical Stance

As with any change in position, the firer will need to build up his techniques through practise and confirm by firing any change in his MPI or size of the Hit Probability Area (HPA).

When using the barricade for support, various techniques can be practised:

1. Place the palm of the weak hand against the post and use the thumb as a hook under the wrist of the firing hand for support.

2. Brace the thumb of the weak hand against the post to steady the hold when firing from the right hand side.

3. Rest the knuckles, wrist or forearm against the post.

4. Grasp the post with the supporting hand and use the wrist to support the wrist of the firing hand.

5. A technique used in the Bianchi shoot when using optical sights, is to place the index finger over the barrel with the lower fingers in front of the lug holding the barricade and the thumb holding against the rear of the barricade. When firing on the right side of the barricade the left hand is used to fire the revolver and when firing on the left side the right hand is used.

Bianchi Grip

A length of metal fitted to the top of the barrel and at a right angle to it (just behind the index finger) may be used as a barricade stop. A finger stop should also be fitted on the top of the barrel (in front of the index finger) to protect it against the blast from the ports and to prevent the finger from moving forward., which could otherwise result in the finger being shot off.

6. This technique may be used with a pistol that has a shroud fitted around the slide and frame in front of the ejection port. The shroud allows the slide to travel back during recoil and offers a degree of safety in the event of a burst barrel.

Each technique may affect the initial movement when releasing the shot due to variations in holding and so the HPA should always be confirmed.

Safety

The author considers this technique to be unsafe and strongly recommends the firer to wear a glove to protect against side blast. The glove, of course, will give no protection against a burst barrel and serious personal injury.

Two Handed Control

Using both hands assists in steadying the handgun and offers greater control of recoil. The degree of control is dependent on the grip used and the stance adopted.

Cup Support

Using the weak hand as a 'cup' improves steadiness but gives little improvement in control (taming the recoil).

Cup Support

Overhand Grip

In this technique, grasp the wrist by placing the thumb over the wrist. The thumb acts as a counter lever to minimise the wrist pivoting during recoil. Care should be taken 'not to take the pulse' which could be transferred into the handgun.

Overhand Grip

Safety

To avoid 'hammer bite', caused when the slide moves back to cock the hammer, the thumb should pull back the flesh of the web between the thumb and trigger finger, ensuring that the thumb is below the slide as it recoils back on the frame.

Slide and Grip Characteristics

The higher the bore line in relation to the grip, the greater the effect of recoil. Some pistols of modern design have overcome hammer bite by raising the height of the slide above the grip and re-contouring the grip tang, for example, the SIG 226. Others have eliminated the hammer using a striker mechanism which is contained within the profile of the pistol, for example, the Glock Pistol.

Glock Pistol

Browning Pistol (top) and SIG Sauer Pistol (bottom)

Note the slide grip characteristics. These two pistols would not be eligible to be used in ARA / SP as they have been modified with the addition of Packmayr grips and replacement sights.

Two Handed Hold

This is achieved by using the indents between the fingers of the firing hand as a 'custom grip' for the controlling hand.

Applying a greater pressure with the controlling hand than that of the firing hand allows the trigger finger to act independently. This technique offers faster recovery of the sight picture after recoil than the cup or the overhand grip, as the hold is forward of the pivoting wrist and so counteracts it.

Two Handed Hold

The natural position for the trigger finger is dictated by the size of the firer's hand (reach) and the width of the pistol grip. This is also applicable when placing the index finger of the non-firing hand on the front of the trigger guard.

A double column magazine makes the grip wider and results in the trigger finger coming into contact with the frame, possibly resulting in disturbing the aim when squeezing the trigger. (This disturbance, which contributes to the initial movement, is usually compensated for when the handgun is zeroed, **providing the disturbance is consistent for each shot**).

To counteract this disturbance, the supporting hand index finger can be placed on the front of the trigger guard. The firer then applies the same pressure with this finger on the trigger guard as the trigger finger on the trigger during firing. In effect he squeezes off two triggers.

Finger on Trigger Guard

Greater recovery of recoil is possible due to 'holding' the fore-end of the trigger guard. To avoid the finger shifting during recoil, the front of the trigger guard should be re-curved and chequered.

This is also the reason why a fore-end grip is fitted to a Section 5 burst fire pistol as seen in the following illustration.

Beretta 3 Shot Burst Fire Pistol

This Beretta 3 shot burst fire pistol has a fore-end grip and detachable shoulder stock to give greater stability when firing. Note the ported barrel.

Left Hand Firing for a Right Hand Firer

If you are a right handed firer and match conditions say you must fire left handed; this following technique may be helpful. Place your left hand trigger finger over the trigger and then place your right hand trigger finger over your left one. Squeeze the trigger by pressing your right finger over your left. This may feel more natural than squeezing off the shot with the weak hand index finger.

This technique is possible if the gun has an elongated winter trigger guard, which is designed to allow the gun to be fired whilst wearing gloves.

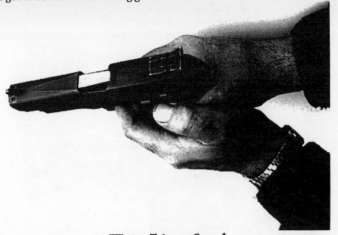

Winter Trigger Guard

Safety (Finger in front of trigger guard)

The firer should not use this technique with a revolver. Spitting lead may be forced out between the cylinder face and the forcing cone of the barrel.

Unsafe Technique with a Revolver

High Grip - Revolver

A technique which may be used on a revolver, to extend the reach and to provide extra leverage to the trigger when firing double action, is to position the hand high on the backstrap. Greater control of recoil can also be achieved as the wrist is closer to the bore line. The trigger finger may be positioned so that when the tip of the finger comes into contact with the frame at the rear of the trigger guard or the thumb. This enables the firer to know precisely when the hammer will fall (do not use this technique to stage the trigger).

The thumb should be kept clear of the cylinder release latch as this may be pushed forward during recoil (Smith & Wesson revolver), possibly releasing the cylinder which would then result in a stoppage. When a large thumb latch has been fitted take extra care so as not to create this problem. With a Colt revolver this problem does not occur as the cylinder release latch has to be moved to the rear to release the cylinder. Neither is it a problem with a Dan Wesson revolver as the latch is in front of the cylinder. This is ideal when unloading the revolver with the weak hand only.

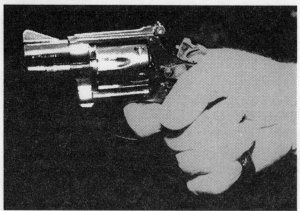

High Grip (Revolver)

High Grip - Pistol

A similar high grip can be obtained on a customised pistol.

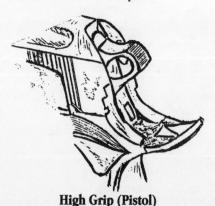

High Grip (Pistol)

A recessed high swept Beavertail tang allows the web between the thumb and trigger finger to sit higher. This also eliminates hammer bite as well as spreading the recoil over a greater area of the hand.

Concaving the underside of the trigger guard, where it joins the frame, also allows the hand to sit higher to the bore line, (this is now a standard feature on a Colt 1911 A1), as does allowing the thumb to rest on the enlarged frame mounted safety catch. It is advisable to fit a thumb guard on pistols which have the slide rail on the outside of the frame to avoid the thumb coming into contact and slowing down the slide in its travel, possibly resulting in a stoppage or minor injury to the thumb which can result in shifting the hand and losing a consistent grip.

Preparation Before Firing

At the end of each handling practise the handgun should be lightly oiled for storage. Do not store it in a leather holster as gun oil can affect the natural oils used to protect the leather.

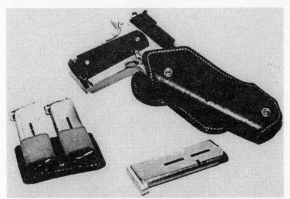

Storing the Handgun

All traces of oil and grease should be removed by dry cleaning the chamber/s and breech face or recoil shield before firing. Any oil or water present will result in increased chamber pressure. Oil and water cannot be compressed, which results in the brass case not being able to expand to form a gas tight seal.

The pressure that is normally used to expand the case is now forcing the bullet down the barrel and the base of the case against the breech face or recoil shield. (Not taking into account the gap between the cylinder face and the forcing cone of the barrel).

Apart from the dangerous implication, the shots will go high, due to the increased pressure. As the oil burns off, shooting becomes erratic and feeding and extraction problems are caused by the build up of carbon.

Wet ammunition also causes increased chamber pressure and erratic shooting as the water vaporises.

Ammunition should be kept out of the direct rays of the sun as this will affect the performance.

The bore should be dry cleaned to ensure that there is no oil or water present. If present this could cause a bulged barrel or shots to go low on the target.

Live Firing & Coaching

Live firing should be supervised by a suitably experienced and qualified coach. The art of coaching is to pass on shooting knowledge gained from previous experience and to offer encouragement during correcting errors in the firer's techniques.

As stated in the introduction, each stage should be mastered before going onto the next. The firer should initially be coached using a small bore handgun, for example a .22 conversion kit in a Colt 1911 A1. This not only keeps the cost of practise down, it also helps in ensuring that the firer does not become 'gun shy'.

Coach's Position

The coach's position during firing should allow him to observe the grip, trigger finger and eye of the person being coached. In the case of a right handed firer with a left master eye, the spotter should move forward, in line with the coach, to observe if the firer is flinching.

Coach and Spotter's Position

Safety

The coach and the spotter, as well as the firer, should always wear safety glasses and ear defenders.

Shooting Glasses and Ear Defenders

Coaching Procedures

The coach should observe the firer for faults in his techniques and not the target. The firer should call each shot, declaring where the sights were in relation to the aiming mark at the moment of firing. The assistant should scope and record each shot as it falls to compare it with the firer's declaration.

The firer should not be distracted during firing; let him concentrate on the essentials of marksmanship and applying his techniques.

Observations should be noted on the record card by the coach and compared with the declaration, when discussing the pattern of the group.

Extreme Spread

The Extreme Spread (ES) is the distance between the two most furthest shots in the group and is used to measure the group size and radius. The Mean Point of Impact (MPI) is the centre of the group. Its displacement should be measured from the aiming mark, Point of Aim (POA), and recorded in the firer's record book.

No attempt should be made to adjust the sights at this time (assuming that the shots are on the target).

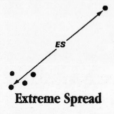

Extreme Spread

A pulled shot can be ignored when measuring the ES, providing that it has been declared correctly and the declaration is confirmed by the assistant scoping the shots. No more than 1 pulled shot should be allowed, when measuring the group size, as this would permit unacceptable inconsistency in the grouping standard. As the firer gains experience of the essentials of marksmanship a pulled shot will become less frequent.

Determine the MPI of the group and its displacement from the aiming mark. The pattern of the group, for example, the shot displacement within the group, will indicate faults in his technique, breathing, etc. The firer should be encouraged to concentrate on each shot as it is released and should be told not to *aim off* the aiming mark in an attempt to hit it. It is only the grouping standard that is important at this stage and not the MPI in relation to the POA.

Factors Affecting the Fall of Shot (Group Patterns)

3 to 9 o' Clock Errors

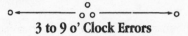

3 to 9 o' Clock Errors

This can be caused by:

Moving position, not maintaining natural alignment, snatching, suddenly releasing the trigger, lateral error in sight alignment and applying inconsistent pressure with the trigger finger/thumb against the grip/frame.

6 to 12 o' Clock Errors

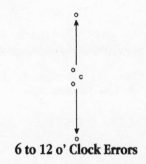

6 to 12 o' Clock Errors

This can be caused by:

Incorrect sight picture (vertical), incorrect eye relief, not controlling breathing, over travel on trigger, little finger applying pressure to the toe of the front strap and applying pressure to the heel of the backstrap with the heel of the hand. (Inconsistent grip).

2 to 8 o' Clock Errors

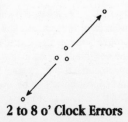

2 to 8 o' Clock Errors

This can be caused by:

Inconsistent grip, head canted and other factors as at 1 and 2.

4 to 10 o' Clock Errors

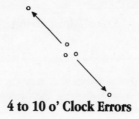

4 to 10 o' Clock Errors

This can be caused by:

Factors as at 1, 2 and 3.

In the event of the group being enlarged for no apparent reason, the coach, after confirming the accuracy of the handgun and ammunition, can then consider aiming errors.

Aiming errors can be confirmed by using a white target with no aiming mark with the firer being instructed to aim at the centre of the unfocused target.

The firer should be reminded that when using open sights, the aiming mark will be blurred when he has obtained the correct sight picture (as there is no aiming mark on the paper target, he has only the sight alignment on which to focus).

Aiming errors can also be confirmed to the firer by fitting an optical sight (red dot) as it is not necessary for him to focus on the sights. Any improvement in his grouping standard can then be directly attributed to not having to align the open sights.

When using a red dot sight both eyes may be kept open to focus on the target. This gives the advantage of depth perception particularly when judging the distance to targets in practical events, to determine the POA. Firers who have difficulty in closing the weak eye can improve their standard of shooting by fitting a red dot sight. (Match conditions permitting).

Alternatively, by fitting a laser beam sight under the barrel, which projects a red laser dot onto the target, the coach can see the area of the aim and any subsequent disturbance when releasing the shot. The firer is obviously encouraged to use the open sights and not the red dot of the laser beam. Ideally, the dot should appear below the firer's line of sight (LOS) / Aiming Mark. Laser sights are now available that fit in place of the recoil spring guide fitted below the barrel, enabling a conventional holster to be used and the index finger of the supporting hand to be positioned on the front of the trigger guard.

Laser Sight on Trigger Guard

Should the firer be remaining in the aim too long, remind him to take an 'area' aim, for example, within a 50 mm radius of the point of aim if necessary, and then fire. If he should have a stoppage or run dry and does not realise it, let him continue. If he is tightening the grip, snatching the trigger or suddenly releasing it or flinching, it will be seen at this time.

Negligent Discharge

During live firing the coach should closely supervise the apprehensive firer. On grasping the trigger on a semi-automatic pistol to fire the shot, the firer may not allow the trigger to travel forward again as the slide moves forward to disengage the disconnector (this device is to stop the pistol from firing on automatic). Because the trigger is still held back and cannot be squeezed any further, he may think he has run dry, only to find that on relaxing, it will fire when he decides to ease springs by dropping the hammer, resulting in a negligent discharge.

Safety

A pistol is only unloaded when the magazine has been removed and the working parts have been retracted. This is so that the chamber and the breech face may be inspected to ensure that the round has been extracted. (It is possible that the extractor claw has overridden the rim on a hard extraction or the ejector has broken).

Initial Movement

It is physically impossible to hold a perfectly steady aim due to the pulse and muscular tremors. Movement can be minimised by remaining calm and in control during releasing the shot.

Do not hyperventilate and raise the heartbeat and pulse rate by breathing in deeply more than once immediately before each string of shots.

The initial movement is further increased by squeezing the trigger to allow the hammer to fall. This drives the firing pin forward to strike the primer, which ignites the propellant (powder). As the gases expand they force the sides of the case against the chamber wall and the base of the case against the breech face/recoil shield to form a gas tight seal. As the pressure continues to increase, the bullet is forced into the barrel to take up the rifling. (The material from which the case is made needs to be ductile as it has to contract, when the pressure is reduced, so as to later allow it to be extracted/ejected. Brass is frequently used due to the elasticity of the drawn metal case).

Barrel Jump

The jump of the barrel, caused by recoil during this time, is minimal, due to the weight of the handgun in relation to the bullet. (This movement is compensated for, when adjusting the sights during zeroing). The jump of the muzzle also accounts for the trajectory's Line of Departure. (LOD). Variations in grip and eye relief usually make it impractical for one individual to zero for another.

Any uncontrolled movement caused by the firer being 'gun shy' will result in his grouping standard being enlarged, as will an inconsistent grip that does not allow the handgun to consistently 'sit back' in the hand for subsequent shots. Ideally, an experienced firer will have perfected his grip during the draw and will maintain it during a string of shots.

Effect of Recoil

As the bullet leaves the barrel, the energy at the muzzle is suddenly released. It is still momentarily forcing the case back against the breech face/recoil shield which continues to move the handgun back in the hand, raising the muzzle higher due to the wrist and elbow pivoting.

As the felt recoil does not occur until after the bullet has left the barrel, any additional movement during the time the bullet is travelling down the barrel is usually caused by the firer being gun shy; for example, flinching (closing the eyes) or jerking the reflexes (tightening the grip) **in anticipation** of the felt recoil.

The coach should observe the less proficient firer during practise. In the event of the gun running dry and the firer not realising it, the coach should say nothing. On firing a dry shot, the firer will realise that the disturbance is entirely due to himself anticipating or exaggerating the recoil. The coach may leave an empty chamber in a revolver or load a snap cap into a magazine to enable this to purposely occur. An unreliable magazine may also be used as it is often considered dangerous to mix live and drill rounds. Note: as the pressure is released as the bullet leaves the muzzle, the slide is unlocked to recoil back on the frame. It is at this time that the 'felt recoil' occurs. (When leaving an empty chamber in a revolver you need to consider the direction of the rotation of the cylinder. A modern Colt revolver rotates clockwise and a Smith & Wesson revolver rotates anticlockwise). Even though the coach may know when the dry shot will be fired it is still advisable for him to maintain the safe distance and position in relation to the firer so as to prevent a serious accident occurring. A friend of mine lost an eye whilst observing a firer when a spent case was ejected. The correct positions for the coach and spotter should be determined by observing the direction and fall of the cases prior to them taking up their positions.

To encourage the firer to stop flinching, have him declare his shots from the sight picture seen on releasing the shot. The coach should observe the firer for any faults, using an assistant to scope/spot the shots, to confirm the declaration, for example, correct, correct, high right.

Follow Through

Providing the firer applies the essentials of marksmanship, using his chosen techniques, the sights will land on or near the POA, allowing a second shot to be fired quickly and accurately (Double Tap). Should the firer's declaration not be consistent with the spotter's observation, have him declare where the sights land after firing the shot as this may at least encourage him to try to keep his eyes open.

Note: where the sights 'land' in relation to the POA will indicate where a pulled shot has been displaced, for example, low left, etc.

Grouping Standards

A 'group' is a series of shots (not less than 3 and usually 5) fired at the same aiming mark, using the same techniques. It requires 3 shots for triangulation; the fourth and fifth are confirmatory shots to establish the group size in the event of one of the first three shots being pulled.

The firer's ability to apply his chosen techniques is seen in his grouping standard. Any variation in position, grip, sight picture or shot release during the initial movement will result in the group being enlarged and/or displaced.

The grouping practise should be fired at 10m using a 50 mm x 50 mm white aiming mark on a black background, to present a clear sight picture.

Point of Aim (POA)

Handgun Grouping Standards at 10 m

25 mm	Tight Grouper
50 mm	Good Grouper
75 mm	Above Average Grouper
100 mm	Average Grouper
125 mm	Poor Grouper

Theory of a Group

In theory the group will expand in direct proportion to the range.

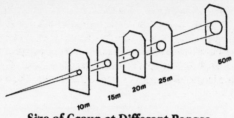

Size of Group at Different Ranges

For clarity the trajectory and drift is not shown. In theory, a 50 mm grouper at 10m should contain his shots inside the following circles at longer ranges.

75 mm	circle at	15 m
100 mm	circle at	20 m
125 mm	circle at	25 m
250 mm	circle at	50 m

Expected Scoring Area

This circle is the area into which the firer may expect his shots to fall and is referred to as the Expected Scoring Area (ESA). In practise, this does not take into consideration the fact that the aiming mark is less easily seen at the longer ranges or the displacement of the MPI for each separate group, should there be any inconsistency in position, grip or eye relief.

Although grouping is the foundation of all shooting, the ability to group tightly is not sufficient on its own to obtain good shooting results.

Unless the firer can consistently place his groups/MPI on the same area of the target, the result will be an increase in the size of his Hit Probability Area (HPA).

To determine the precise error caused by variations in position, eye relief or inconsistent grip, the zeroing procedure should be carried out.

Zeroing Procedure

With 6 rounds, load and make ready, test and adjust onto the aiming mark and fire 3 shots.

Activate the safety device (if fitted) and lay the handgun on the shooting bench, pointing down the range.

Step back to break the position and then forward again to take up the handgun and fire the remaining 3 shots. (After first testing and adjusting the position).

Re--load and repeat the practice again for a total of 12 shots.

During the zeroing procedure it will probably be found that the inexperienced firer's group size will expand due to the variations in his position, hold and eye relief, etc, for each 3 round group.

Providing that the 12 round group size does not expand greater than 50% of his grouping standard, (for example, a 50 mm grouper's ESA should not expand to greater than 75m), the firer has proved that he has achieved reasonable consistency in group placement on the target, ie he has the ability to adopt the same position and hold when firing. When this is achieved, the sights can be adjusted to move the MPI onto the centre of the aiming mark. This is zeroing the weapon.

The firer who has not achieved consistency in group placement when using the same techniques and aiming mark will have to accept that he cannot precisely zero his handgun. This lack of precision can be measured.

After the sights have been adjusted, fire a 5 shot check group. Providing that the MPI of the check group is within 25% of this group size from the POA, the handgun should be considered as zeroed.

Any further attempt to adjust the sights, until the firer has achieved consistency in group placement, will result in chasing the error, by not knowing which group/MPI to adjust from.

Displacement of Groups

The displacement of groups, as illustrated above, shows the enlarged mean group size, (HPA), of four, separate groups of three rounds each. The black centre represents the POA.

Hit Probability Area (HPA)

This is the area into which a single shot can realistically be expected to fall and is dependent on a number of factors. In practical terms, the firer's hit probability area (HPA) at 10m is more likely to be related to the displacement of the MPI of each group rather than each 3 or 5 round group size. It will probably be found that a pulled shot from within the firer's 3 or 5 round grouping standard is within his enlarged HPA.

A firer with an HPA of 100 mm at 10m will miss with some of his shots when engaging a man size target at 50m because his HPA will have expanded to 500 mm, which is wider than the width of the target.

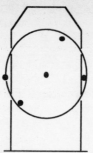

HPA at 50m (Target 450 mm Wide)

Factors Affecting the HPA

Zeroing Error

In the case of a proficient grouper, (who can consistently contain his 12 round group in a 75 mm circle at 10m), no error should be permitted after adjusting the sights, as this will displace the MPI/HPA in proportion to the range.

Example

Leaving a 15 mm MPI error on the sights when zeroing at 10m will displace the MPI/HPA by 75 mm at 50m as the angle of error increases in proportion to the range.

Zeroing is carried out to adjust the sights to move the MPI into the centre of the bull, in relation to the POA using the chosen stance.

To calculate the amount of sight adjustment required, divide the range in millimetres (mm) by the sight base in mm, for example, range (10m) 10,000 mm divided by a sight base of 200 mm equals 50 mm. Therefore, adjusting the sight by 1 mm will move the MPI by 50 mm; adjusting the sight by 1.5 mm will move the MPI by 75 mm.

Sight Adjustment

Move the foresight in the direction of the error by drifting the foresight towards the displaced MPI or by changing it for a lower or higher one. Alternatively, adjust the rear sight away from the error. (In the direction you want the group to move).

After adjusting the sights, they may be secured in place to hold zero by using two rubber buffers. These allow any minor adjustments to be made, yet prevent the sights being moved by 'whiplash' during recoil.

Stabilising the Adjustable Rear Sight

Minute of Angle (MOA) at 10m and 50m

Adjusting the sights by 1 mm will move the MPI by approximately 66 mm at 10m with a 5" barrel semi-automatic pistol and approximately 50 mm with a 6" revolver. Adjusting the sights by 1 mm when firing from 50m will move the MPI by 330 mm and 250 mm respectively.

Note: a 1 mm sight alignment error has the same effect, ie, moving the MPI,

Speed of Engagement

It may be found that, when engaging the target during the rapid practices, for example, SPB Practice 4, PP2 Practice 1, the HPA may be displaced. The firer should confirm any change to his MPI which is affected by the speed of engagement as it may differ from his MPI obtained during the more leisurely deliberate zeroing procedure. The firer should check the placement of his trigger finger to ensure that it always remains consistent during the rapid practice.

Change In Position

After zeroing, the firer should confirm his HPA for changes in position and record the POA in his record book.

Example

At 50m, it may be found when firing from the left hand barricade the POA needs to be the edge of the target in order to ensure that the HPA/MPI is centred.

The prone, kneeling and sitting positions offer greater stability than the standing position as there are at least three points of contact with the ground.

The coach should encourage the firer to practise adopting these positions in order to build up the muscles and to master the techniques.

The firer should then 'comfortably' achieve results which are at least as good as those achieved in the standing position at the same range.

To maintain consistency in eye relief, the upper body should be the same as, or as near as possible to, the stance used when zeroing.

Prone Techniques

In some disciplines the firer is required to lie on the ground and adopt the prone position. The prone positions illustrated have similar features to the stance used when zeroing.

Prone Isosceles

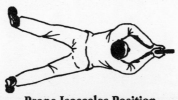

Prone Isosceles Position

Prone Weaver

Prone Weaver Position

Bending the knee rolls the body over slightly; this then takes the weight off the stomach and chest which assists breathing. It also raises the head and avoids impeding vision caused by squinting out of the top of the eye and straining in the aim. To raise the line of sight, a longer grip may be fitted on a revolver or an extended magazine inserted into a pistol, if match conditions permit.

To avoid any major displacement/expansion of the HPA, the butt should not be rested on hard ground; use the flesh on the heel of the controlling hand to cushion the initial movement.

Grip Extension

When using a standard handgun without a grip extension, the head may be rested on the upper arm. This technique requires the head to be canted, which in practical terms is better than holding the head back and straining the neck. This technique may also be adopted when using the kneeling and sitting position, providing the firer is 'comfortable'. Wearing ear defenders with large cups allows the head to be rested on the upper arm to gain additional stability.

Kneeling Techniques

Elbow on knee, sitting on foot.
Similar to Weaver. Do not allow the knee bone and elbow to come into contact as it is unstable. Use the indent above the elbow or knee, depending on the elevation required.

Kneeling Position

Note the outstretched arm for maximum eye relief.

Kneeling on both knees.
Upper body as per the Isosceles or Weaver position.

Arms outstretched.
Similar to Isosceles position.

Sitting Techniques

Elbows on knees.
Both elbows on knees. The position should be oblique to the line of fire. Similar to Weaver.

Knee raised.
To lock in with wrists. Similar to Isosceles.

Sitting Position

Changes in Elevation in Relation to the Target

The point of aim, POA, should always be confirmed where the line of departure (LOD) is changed due to the fall or rise of the ground. This is because the trajectory of the bullet is changed by the change in the LOD.

Changes in Light Conditions

Any changes in light conditions can result in the firer not applying his HPA to the centre of the target. On a dull day, the aiming mark is less easily seen, leading the firer to aim lower in order to see it more clearly.

On a bright day the aiming mark appears more clearly and there is a tendency to aim higher into it without considering the affect of trajectory at longer ranges.

A more common occurrence is that the light being reflected off the foresight, (possibly due to holster wear), may result in the firer not seeing part of it clearly, as the eye is attracted to the strongest source of light. This results in aiming off. (Consider the affect of a 1 mm sight alignment error using blurred sights).

Sight Black Equipment

To minimise unwanted reflection of light off the sights, it is recommended that the sights are blackened. Do not use ordinary paint. Sights can be blackened by either temporarily spraying the sights with special 'sight black' paint, which is a very fine carbon-based paint, or by depositing a very thin film of carbide soot , which provides the ideal non-reflective mat black sight picture.

Acetylene Sight Black Equipment

Gas is produced by adding water to calcium carbide in a small lamp; this is then lit and the sights held above the flame in order to deposit the soot.

Acetylene Sight Black Equipment

In competitions, open front holsters are used to prevent the soot from being wiped off the front sight during the draw. Ideally a standard enclosed holster should have a sight track incorporated into the design for the same purpose. Between stages of shooting, when patching out, etc, the rear sight can be protected from being wiped clean by covering it with a hood. This can be made by cutting a plastic 35 mm film container.

Open Front Holster

Wind Effect

Wind effect is minimal on a bullet when short ranges are used. However, what does affect the fall of shot is the stability of the position. Wherever possible, during the deliberate stages, engage the target between gusts of wind.

Braced Position

Note the braced position of the firer on the right.

The inexperienced firer's performance deteriorates rapidly in adverse weather conditions, especially when he sees some of his early results.

The proficient firer knows that the conditions are probably going to affect his HPA and braces himself, expecting it to expand. This enables him to retain a degree of confidence in applying the enlarged HPA to the centre of the target.

Rifling Twist

When engaging targets at longer ranges the drift of the bullet caused by the rifling twist must be considered. This can be illustrated on a black 1500 target. It will be seen that the X-Ring on this target is offset to the right, as shown in a following illustration. The firer can use the centre of the neck as a POA at 50m as it presents a clearer sight picture because of the white on either side of the neck. Handguns are used with pre-set adjustable sights for 7, 25 and 50m to enable the firer to quickly adjust the sights.

Sight Adjustment

The foresight can be adjusted for height by moving the cam along the ramp.

Pre-set Adjustable Sights

A technique that may be used with pre-set adjustable sights is to adjust the sight to enable the white 'figure 9' above the bull (not shown in the illustration) to be used as the aiming mark at 10m with the sight set at 7m and the MPI falling into the X-Ring below. This distinct POA avoids being distracted by the shots falling below the LOS. At 15m the sight may be set at 25m, to take a central POA on the shot holes in the X-Ring. This is the POA and sight setting used when the handgun was zeroed, and may be referred to as the correct zeroing point (CZP). The light passing from behind the target, through the X-Ring, presents a clear sight picture at 15m. At 25m the POA with the sight set at 25m will probably be found to be below the X-Ring, due to the trajectory. The POA at 50m is as previously described.

Rifling Drift

If using a handgun which has a right hand twist, for example, a Smith & Wesson, the bullet will drift to the right towards the X-Ring. A .38 Special bullet will drift approximately 25 mm (1 inch) at 50 metres. The Colt has a left hand rifling twist and so the drift will be to the left. This is one of the reasons why Smith & Wesson handguns are more popular in this discipline.

When using a handgun without pre-set adjustable sights which has been zeroed at 10m with downloaded ammunition, the Point of Aim should be approximately 150 mm (6") above the X-Ring at 50 meters to allow for the trajectory or fall of shot.

In this event, the rifling drift should be considered when adjusting the sight laterally or when selecting the POA when firing at longer ranges. Rifling drift is often mistakenly attributed to wind or light conditions.

The drift should be confirmed in long range pistol (and rifle disciplines) on a calm day from a rested position.

X-Ring, Ensuring the Target is Vertical

Note the offset of the X-Ring in relation to the centre of the neck. Use a Plumb Bob to ensure that the target is vertical.

To further illustrate the affect of drift at longer ranges, consider the design of the 1878 Colt Double Rifle. Each side by side barrel has an opposite rifling twist so that the MPIs are superimposed at 100 yards.

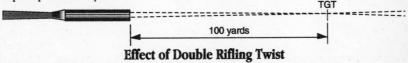

Effect of Double Rifling Twist

Note that the MPIs converge at 100 yards and start to diverge past this distance. This factor needs to be considered when firing at longer ranges.

Trajectory

The bullet starts to fall as soon as it leaves the barrel. This is compensated for by the elevation of the Line of Bore (LOB) in relation to the Line of Sight (LOS) and is achieved by adjusting the sights. The 'jump' caused by the initial movement also effects the line of departure (LOD) of the bullet. This enables the bullet to rise and strike the LOS at a pre-determined zeroing distance, for example, at 10m.

In practical terms when using service ammunition, this results in the shot going higher at longer ranges up to 25m until the bullet has reached its Culminating Point (CP). This is just over half the distance it will have to travel before striking the LOS again.

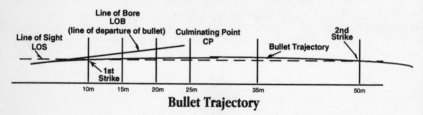

Bullet Trajectory

The height of the CP above the LOS is dependent on the flat shooting characteristics of the ammunition (velocity of the round). The higher the velocity, the harder the handgun will sit back in the hand, resulting in increasing the initial movement. This in turn pivots the wrist and raises the LOB. You will see in the previous illustration that the MPI at 15m, whilst rising, is the same 'height' at 35m, whilst falling. In the Bianchi event targets have to be engaged at 35 yards. The POA should be approximately the same height at 35 yards as the 15 yard POA for this reason.

Points of Aim to Compensate for Trajectory

It may be found in the prone and sitting positions that a lower POA is required as the Line of Departure (LOD) is raised. Owing to the firer's lower position, the trajectory of the bullet will be altered from that of the standing position.

Trigger Guard - PAA (Police Athletic Association) Target

On a Police Athletic Association (PAA) target the trigger finger, which is the centre of the X-Ring, should be used as the POA at 10m. The lower fingers should progressively be used for the POA as the range increases up to 25m. This allows the foresight tip to be focused on the white of the target.

Yellow Wrist - Fig 11 Target

In Service Pistol, using a figure 11 target, when considering the trajectory, the top of the wrist on a Fig 11 target should be the POA at 10m with the MPI of the group falling on the bottom of the wrist (centre of the bull). This permits the POA to be progressively lowered into the wrist at longer ranges, for example, 15m, 20m and 25m, to enable the tip of the foresight to be focused against the yellow wrist.

Selecting a new Point of Aim (POA) will lower the trajectory (MPI) and raise the results.

Points of Aim for Changes in Trajectory

The new figure 11 targets make no allowance in the height of the scoring areas as it uses scoring rings instead of rectangles. The old bull was approximately 50 mm wide x 100 mm high, whilst the new is 75 mm in diameter.

 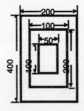

Old and New Fig 11 Targets (Service Pistol Targets)

It will be seen from the previous illustrations that it is no longer feasible to take the same POA previously possible when using a rectangular bull as it was more forgiving in height.

Practical Pistol, Western and Bianchi targets are buff coloured with no disruptive pattern, enabling a clear sight picture to be obtained. Speed Action Plates are white which gives a clear sight picture.

Service handguns, which have fixed sights, are usually factory zeroed to give an MPI at 50m with service ammunition. This enables the POA at 20m to be in the white at 6 o'clock, just under the bull, on a standard black bullseye target.

The firer will need to confirm the POA in practise, with the batch of ammunition being used whilst concentrating on the sight picture when releasing the shot in the centre of the unfocused POA.

Application of Fire Practices

Application of fire is to place the MPI/HPA onto the highest scoring area on the target, which is usually in the centre; in order to gain maximum scores.

There are exceptions to this, for example when engaging steel plates that fall when hit, in the Man v Man at Bisley where they are positioned out to 35 yds or elongated 'pepper popper' practical pistol targets.

The MPI should be higher to impart sufficient energy to knock the target past its fulcrum point. When set up, these type of targets are usually laid slightly forward which results in low shots within the firer's HPA being deflected down towards the hinge.

To confirm factors affecting the HPA , a number of check groups should be fired. (Similar to the 12 round zeroing procedure). To achieve this, the firer's grouping standard needs to be confirmed in each position which is to be used. Only when he has achieved consistency in group placement on the target using the same POA, should the new POA be recorded in the firer's record book. These should be reconfirmed during match practise with the cadence (speed) of fire being used. It must be appreciated that shooting practise/dry firing must be carried out on a regular basis if the firer is to achieve the consistency to become a marksman.

Sighting Shots

The firer should not be drawn to alter his POA for shots that fall within his HPA, neither should he change his POA or adjust the sights on his first shot or a pulled shot.

Example

In PP2 five sighting shots at 50m are permitted. Assuming the firer's HPA at 25m is 150 mm in the kneeling position and there is no displacement of the MPI caused by the change in position or range, in theory it will expand to 300 mm at 50m. A shot should therefore fall within a 150 mm radius from the POA due to the random dispersal of the group.

150 mm Radius (300 mm Group)

Consider the consequences of changing the POA after scoping the first shot; the firer, believing he is shooting low left decides to aim high right for the four remaining shots. He would therefore move his HPA away from the centre of the target and from the highest scoring area. An inexperienced firer may often be observed 'chasing the error' after each shot.

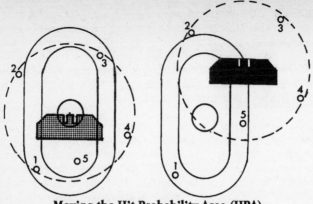

Moving the Hit Probability Area (HPA)

The above illustration shows the result of changing the point of aim after observing the first shot. The HPA has now moved away from the centre of the target.

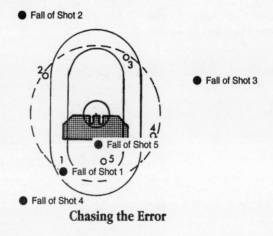

Chasing the Error

The above illustration shows the result of changing the point of aim after observing each displaced shot. The black dots represent the Fall of Shot when chasing the error.

Shooting Record Card

Firer's Name: .... **Coach**: .... **Date**: ....

Firearm	❏ Handgun ❏ Rifle	**Model**: ....

Ammunition Details and Load: ....

Discipline	❏ Service ❏ Police	❏ Practical	❏ Bianchi	❏ Rifle
	❏ Long Range Pistol	❏ Other............................		
Stance	❏ Duelling ❏ Isosceles	❏ Weaver	❏ Tactical	❏ ....
Position	❏ Kneeling ❏ Sitting	❏ Prone	❏ Bipod	❏ Standing
	❏ Hawkins ❏ Reclined	❏ L/H Bar	❏ R/H Bar	❏ Lug/Stop

Range	❏ Metres	❏ Yards	❏ Location			
	❏ 10	❏ 15	❏ 20	❏ 25	❏ 35	❏ 50
	❏ 100	❏ 200	❏ 300	❏ 400	❏ 500	❏ 600

Target	❏ Static	❏ Walking	❏ Jogging	❏ Running	
Confirming	❏ MPI	❏ POA	❏ HPA	❏ Lead	❏ Group Size ......
Light	❏ Bright	❏ Dull	**Time**	.... am / pm	

Wind Strength (Speed)	❏ Mild 5-10 mph	❏ Fresh 10-15 mph	❏ Strong 15-20 mph	
Wind Bearing		❏ 30°	❏ 45°	❏ 60° ❏ 90°
Wind Direction		❏ Left	❏ Right	
Rifling Twist/Drift		❏ Left	❏ Right	mm: ....

Sight Adj (No. of Clicks)   Left: ....   Right: ....   Up: ....   Down: ....

Target

Notes

Cleaning After Firing

The military explanation for barrel corrosion is that it is caused by the hot gases being forced into the pores of the metal. As the gases cool they 'weep out' and deposit moisture inside the bore, (this is commonly called 'sweating'). This causes rust which then eats into the metal to cause pitting. It is not sufficient to only clean the bore after firing: it must also be inspected on a regular basis to guard against this occurrence. This makes it impractical to store certificate holders' firearms in a central location where access is restricted.

Corrosion can result in the bullet 'yawing', particularly where the rifling meets the forcing cone at the breech end of the barrel or the crown of the barrel at the muzzle end.

Incorrect use of the cleaning rod will also damage the bore.

Erratic Shooting

A bullet often yaws a little after leaving the muzzle and then stabilises in flight. Should the bullet be distorted by the erosion of the lands of the rifling and not spin on its axis after a short time in flight, it may tumble and possibly hit the target broadside on. This is commonly called 'key holing'.

A leaded barrel, which is caused by soft lead being stripped off by the rifling or through a loss of velocity caused by using downloaded ammunition not imparting sufficient speed of spin, also results in key holing.

Disciplines, Courses of Fire and Coaching Information

Courses of fire change with range rules and amendments to Match Conditions. The following information is given as a guide only, so as to enable the coach to prepare an interesting and progressive shooting programme.

With the exception of the Army Rifle Association, civilian competitors can obtain amendments and further information on each discipline by joining the relevant association, a list of which is given at the rear of the book.

Army Rifle Association (ARA) Service Pistol (SP)

The ARA, SP match is fired using a 9 mm pistol as issued to HM Forces or Commonwealth Services. The pistol has to pass Weapons Control to be checked for serviceability and to ensure that the trigger pressure has not been reduced. Privately owned pistols may be used providing they are as issued, including internal parts, for example, the barrel, trigger mechanism and springs.

Service ammunition is issued to competitors on production of a Squadding Card. Firers have been disqualified and banned for life from entering Bisley because of cheating by using other than service ammunition in order to gain an unfair advantage.

ARA, SP consists of 5 Practices, each designed to be more practical than the previous Service Pistol match. This consisted of 4 Practices where the firer was required to load with 6 rounds only in each practice. Prior to this it had been the Service Revolver Match.

National Pistol Association (NPA)

The NPA adopted the old course of fire and designated it Service Pistol B (SPB) in which any handgun from .354 to .455 calibre could be used. They later re-introduced the original match and restricted it to the 9 mm Browning as issued. Factory or reloaded ammunition may be used. This match is designated as SPB (Restricted).

Service Pistol B (SPB)

Practice	Position	Range	Rounds	Targets	Exposures	Procedure
1	Standing	25m	6	1 x Fig 11	1 x 15 secs	6 shots
2	Standing	20m	6	2 x Fig 11	1 x 10 secs	3 shots on each target
3	Standing	15m	6	1 x Fig 11	3 x 3 secs	2 shots per exposure
4	Standing	10m	6	2 x Fig 11	1 x 6 secs	3 shots on each target

In each practice, the firer is ordered to 'Load and make ready'. The firer should test and adjust onto his target/s. This gives the firer the opportunity to perfect his grip and to test his position in order to obtain natural pointing. The firers are then asked 'Is anyone not ready?' before being given the order to 'Watch out! Watch out!'.

The ARA SP course of fire is more practical, consisting of 4 Practices of 10 rounds and 1 Practice of 20.

National Rifle Association (NRA)

The National Rifle Association (NRA) use the ARA, SP Match as their course of fire (Practices 1 to 4 only). Service ammunition is issued on production of a Squadding Card at the Imperial Meeting for the Service Pistol Cup or the Whitehead Inter Service Pistol Match at Bisley, which includes an 8 man civilian team.

The National Pistol Association, NPA, designate this match NRA/SPA and, at the present time, restrict it to the 9 mm Browning as issued, although this will probably be changed to include other service pistols. Service ammunition need not be used. The match is also fired using any handgun from .354 to .455 and is designated by the NPA as SPA Open.

Service Pistol A (SPA)

In Service Pistol A (SPA), the firer has to engage targets from the kneeling, sitting and standing positions. He is no longer permitted time to perfect the grip or to test his position, as is the case in SPB.

Ammunition and Target Requirements
The firer starts the practice with 4 magazines of 10 rounds each. Fig 11 targets are used.

Practice 1
The firer adopts the kneeling position at 25m and is ordered to load and make ready. 2 x Fig 11 targets with 2 exposures of 15 seconds, targets away for 10 seconds in between.

Procedure
On the appearance of the targets engage the Left target with 5 rounds from the kneeling position.

During the 10 seconds whilst the targets are away activate the safety device and adopt the sitting position.

On the re-appearance of the targets engage the Right target with 5 rounds.

Practice 2
The firer adopts the standing position at 25m, pistol loaded (not made ready) and holstered, 1 exposure of 8 seconds, followed by 4 exposures of 3 seconds.

Procedure
On the appearance of the targets for 8 seconds advance to the 20m firing line.

Draw and make ready and engage the left target with 2 rounds.

The left target should be engaged with 2 rounds during each of the 4 exposures of 3 seconds, with the firer returning to the alert position between exposures.

Practice 3
The firer adopts the standing position at 20m, pistol loaded (not made ready) and holstered, 1 exposure of 1 second, followed by 5 exposures of 3 seconds.

Procedure
On the appearance of the 2 x Fig 11 targets for 1 second, advance to the 15m firing line.

Draw, make ready and engage each target with 1 round during each 3 second exposure.

Practice 4
The firer adopts the standing position at 15m, pistol loaded (not made ready) and holstered, 1 exposure of 8 seconds, followed by 2 exposures of 3 seconds of 2 x Fig 11 targets.

Procedure
On the appearance of the targets for 8 seconds advance to the 10m firing line, draw, make ready and engage the targets.

The firer will then receive 2 exposures of 3 seconds. No more than 5 rounds are to count on each target. As any number of rounds may be fired during each exposure, the author prefers to fire 5 rounds on the first (8 second exposure) on the left hand target, 2 rounds on the second exposure on the right hand target and 3 on the third exposure on the right hand target. This avoids having to switch fire between targets during an exposure.

Safety Considerations in Service Pistol A

In Practice 1
The firer's legs and feet may be in front of the pistol whilst in the sitting position. The pistol must be kept pointing down range, parallel to the ground with the safety device applied, when moving from the kneeling position.

In Practices 2, 3 & 4
1. The pistol cannot be drawn and made ready until the firer is on the firing point.

2. The hand must not be used to retain the handgun in its holster during movement. Dropping the handgun will result in disqualification.

3. The firer must return to the standing alert position between exposures. (Bend the elbows to lower the pistol to be parallel to the ground, pointing in the direction of the targets). The safety catch need not be applied between exposures.

4. Only firers who have attained a high standard of gun handling and shooting ability should progress from SPB to SPA.

Dangerous Practice in Service Pistol A

All firers and members of the safety staff should be briefed by the conducting officer on the action to be taken in the event of a firer drawing a pistol and making ready before reaching the firing point. (The hammer on a revolver must not be cocked whilst moving down range). The action will usually be either:

1. The firers are ordered to stop. The individual who has committed the dangerous practise is ordered to unload and show clear. He is then disqualified from the match.

2. Service personnel in ARA/SP may be allowed to continue the advance. This is at the discretion of the Range Officer as it may be less dangerous to allow the firer to continue the advance onto the firing point so that he is in line with the other firers before being stopped.

Firing Positions in Service Pistol A

As in SPB there are two basic stances the firer can adopt.

1. The Isosceles

2. The Weaver

Each one can be modified to suit the firer's build. The chosen technique will be correct when the firer is comfortable and pointing naturally at the target without straining.

In SPA Practice 1, the firer has to engage targets in the kneeling and sitting positions.

Kneeling on both knees is not permitted by the match conditions. In the sitting position, both buttocks must be in contact with the ground.

In Practices 2,3 and 4, the firer has to make ready in the standing position, after advancing down the range onto the firing point and drawing from the holster. He is no longer permitted time to perfect the grip or to test and adjust the position so as to obtain natural pointing.

Example
In Practice 3, on the appearance of the 2 x Fig 11 targets for 1 second, the firer has 5 seconds in which to advance to the 15m firing point, draw and make ready, before the targets are exposed for 3 seconds; during which time he fires 1 shot at each target.

During training, the firer should confirm the start position of the feet and the length of the paces, to ensure that when arriving on the firing line the position of his feet are correct for his adopted stance: pointing naturally at the target.

It will be found that if the firer moves his feet after arriving on the firing line he will probably over adjust and not gain natural pointing. Bending the knee/s is a quicker and a more precise technique to align the upper body on the first exposure. The position can then be adjusted by moving the feet in the time that the target is turned away (3 - 10 secs) before the next exposure.

The draw must be practised until a consistent grip becomes instinctive. As the pistol is raised to come up into the aim, grasp the slide, allowing the forward movement of the draw to pull it back to the extent of its travel.

Release the slide as the arms are extended with the supporting hand taking up a two handed hold. Breath out while extending the arm/s. Keeping both eyes open allows the optical illusion to occur, enabling the target/POA to be 'seen' through the hands and pistol. Any final adjustments can be made at this time by bending the knees as the first pressure is taken up on the trigger.

Close the weak eye to concentrate on the sight picture and squeeze the trigger. After releasing the first shot on the left hand target, bend the knees to align the upper body with the second target. On releasing this shot, quickly adjust onto the edge of the first target, to confirm alignment, before returning to the alert position for the next exposure. During training the firer should confirm which is the natural direction to traverse when engaging multiple targets. It will generally be found that the right handed firer prefers to engage targets from left to right. Opening the weak eye will 'rest' the master eye between exposures.

Standing Alert Position

Ensure that the alert position is adopted before the next exposure so as not to be penalised for remaining in the aim. Even if the firer is not actually penalised he will still be distracted when the range staff tell him to adopt the alert position.

In SPA Open, the match has been modified to allow the firer to use a revolver or a pistol with a capacity of less than 10 rounds to shoot Practices 1, 2, 3 and 4. When to reload should be confirmed during match practise and recorded in the firer's notes. For example, start Practise 1 with a magazine of 6 rounds and reload with a magazine of 4 rounds; this avoids having to make ready after reloading, during the 10 seconds that the targets are turned away.

ARA Service Pistol Practice 5

This practice can only be fired by service personnel who have attained a high standard of weapon handling and personal shooting ability. Civilians are not allowed to fire this practice.

It is a continuous fire and movement practice consisting of 4 phases. The firer initially stands at 25m, with the pistol loaded (not made ready) and holstered.

Ammunition and Target Requirements
The firer starts the practice with 2 magazines, one of 13 rounds and one of 7. (He is not told when to reload). Fig 11 targets are used.

Phase 1
On the appearance of 4 x Fig 11 targets for 15 seconds, draw, make ready, adopt the kneeling position and engage target number 1 with 4 rounds.

Activate the safety device and adopt the standing alert position.

Phase 2
On receiving a 1 second exposure, advance to the 20m firing point.

10 seconds after the 1 second exposure the targets will be exposed 3 times for 3 seconds.

2 rounds are fired during each 3 second exposure on target number 2. Return to the alert position between exposures. Activate the safety device after the last exposure.

Phase 3
On receiving a 1 second exposure, advance to the 15m firing point and adopt the alert position.

10 seconds after the 1 second exposure the targets will be exposed for 15 seconds.

Fire 2 rounds at targets 2, 3 and 4 then activate the safety catch and adopt the alert position.

Phase 4
On receiving a 1 second exposure advance to the 10m firing point and adopt the alert position.

10 seconds after the 1 second exposure the targets will be exposed for 4 seconds.

Engage target numbers 3 and 4 with 2 rounds on each target.

Unload and show clear.

No more than   4 shots on number 1 target are to count.
               8 shots on number 2 target are to count.
               4 shots on number 3 target are to count.
               4 shots on number 4 target are to count.

If there are more shots on a target, the highest scoring shots will be discounted

Procedure

Start the practice with the magazine of 13 rounds. Using 4 rounds for phase 1 and 6 rounds for phase 2, leaving 3 rounds to commence phase 3.

On the appearance of the targets for 15 seconds, advance to the 15m firing point and fire 2 rounds at target number 2. Remove the magazine, leaving a round in the chamber to avoid having to make ready again. Match conditions state that the magazines must be returned to the pocket or pouch.

Reload with the magazine of 7 rounds and engage targets 3 and 4 with 2 rounds on each. Activate the safety device and adopt the alert position, ready to move on to phase 4.

Using this technique is more practical as it avoids having to reload between exposures. If you started the practice with a 7 round magazine it would require a magazine change, returning the empty magazine to the pocket or pouch after the first exposure on phase 2; all in possibly 3 seconds!

It can be seen from the above practices, phases and procedures, which have to be carried out in this competition; not only is the firer required to be a proficient shot, but he must also be totally familiar with the match conditions and course of fire.

Safety Considerations in Practice 5

Service personnel in Practice 5 are permitted to be made ready when advancing down the range with the finger outside of the trigger guard and the safety device activated.

Should the firer have a stoppage (jam) and is not able to clear it before the next phase starts, he is to place the pistol on the ground, pointing in the direction of the target, and stand back.

The pistol is to be cleared at the end of the practice after the range is cleared.

Range rules and restrictions do not permit civilians to advance down the range with a handgun made ready, with the possible exception of Practical Pistol, when only one firer is going through an assault course or house clearing.

Police Pistol One (PP1)

Police Pistol One (PP1) is similar to SPB in that all stages are fired in the standing position. (At a single PAA target). Any full bore handgun from a .354 to a .455 calibre may be used. Revolvers are the most popular as ammunition can be 'down loaded' so as to give less recoil. (Note that reduced loads in semi automatic pistols also require the recoil spring to be weakened or reduced so as to ensure that the ammunition can cycle the action).

Hand loading 'soft loads' also keeps the cost of ammunition down, although it does raise the trajectory.

The scoring areas on the PAA target are greater in height than the width but the centre X-Ring is circular.

The PAA target is purposely designed so as not to give a distinct aiming mark. This is of little consequence, providing the firer is aiming centrally whilst concentrating on the foresight tip in the rear sight notch. (The target will be blurred). Competitions can also be fired using optical sights.

PP1 has evolved from an old police course of fire called the Mander. 6 rounds are now loaded instead of 5. With vintage revolvers the hammer was rested on an empty chamber. Only revolvers of modern manufacture which allows the hammer to be 'rested' safely, should be used when loading with 6 rounds.

From its introduction there has been a considerable increase in the use of custom handguns rather than the 'as issued' models. Competitions should be organised for 'as issued' handguns to ensure that a variation is obtained.

Course of Fire

The firer starts each practice loaded and made ready. He is given the opportunity to test his position before being given the order to 'Watch & Shoot'. Each practice starts from the ready position.

Practice 1
The firer standing at 25m receives 1 exposure for 2 minutes and engages the target with 6 rounds, reloads and fires a further 6 rounds. No more than 6 rounds may be loaded at any time. No extra time is allowed for reloading.

Practice 2
The firer standing at 15m receives 6 exposures of 2 seconds with the target edging for 5 seconds between exposures, he engages the target with 1 shot during each exposure.

Reload with 6 rounds and the practice is repeated for a total of 12 rounds.

Practice 3
The firer standing at 10m, receives 3 exposures of 2 seconds, he engages the target with 2 shots during each exposure.

Ready Position
The arms should be at 45 degrees, with the handgun pointing to the ground. The hammer may be cocked; the trigger finger should be outside the trigger guard.

Ready Position

The 'ready position' should not be confused with the 'load and make ready position', when the handgun must point in the direction of the target.

Double v Single Action Shooting

It is possible to shoot PP1 with a single action revolver but due to the speed of engagement, the time required to thumb back the hammer wastes valuable time in Practices 2 and 3. It may also result in a change of grip. (The thumb of the weak hand should be used to cock the hammer if firing single action).

If the firer decides to use single action for Practice 1 and then double action for Practices 2 and 3, he should confirm, during training, any change in the HPA for the change in his grip. (Even with experienced firers this is often forgotten when under pressure or competition stress). To obtain consistency in trigger pressure it is therefore more feasible to use double action throughout the whole of the match with a revolver, or alternatively use a semi-automatic single action pistol.

Police Pistol Two (PP2)

Police Pistol Two (PP2) is an advanced course of fire in which the firer has to draw from the holster. Revolvers are holstered and loaded with the hammer down. Pistols are holstered and loaded, but not made ready, however, the hammer may be cocked (with no round in the chamber) to ease racking back of the pistol slide.

Course of Fire

6 Sighting shots in 5 minutes from 50m. The shots may be scoped.

Practice 1
The firer at 10m fires 6 shots in 5 seconds after drawing from the holster. Reload and repeat the practice.

A proficient firer can draw and fire the first shot within 1.5 secs accurately. This is the standard which must be aimed for if the remaining five shots in the string are to be fired accurately in the remaining 3.5 secs.

Practice 2

The firer at 50m fires 24 rounds in 3 minutes, 6 rounds prone, 6 rounds kneeling or sitting. (Kneeling and sitting could be used if it is not possible to fire from the prone position). 6 rounds standing left hand barricade, 6 rounds standing right hand barricade. (Reloading must be completed before changing positions).

Practice 3

The firer at 25m fires 24 rounds in 2 minutes, 6 rounds standing, 6 rounds kneeling, 6 rounds standing right hand barricade, 6 rounds standing left hand barricade.

Match Conditions

When engaging the target from the right of the barricade, the right hand must be used as the firing hand. When firing from the left of the barricade, the left hand must be used as the firing hand.

As both of these positions simulate firing around cover, (foot fault lines dictate the position of the feet), it may be necessary to change or modify the stance and the POA.

In competitions, use the 5 sighting shots to confirm any changes in light conditions and trajectory, in the event the ground/LOS, rising or falling between the firing points and the target.

Safety Considerations in PP2

On a number of ranges, firing from the prone position is not permitted as the line of departure may not be covered by the safety certificate; Quadrant Elevation (QE) of 50 mils (2.8°). In the event of this, the course of fire would have to be modified, for example, use the sitting position.

On ranges where it is permitted, the weapon must be drawn before adopting the position, as the handgun will be pointing **behind** the firing line.

Fifteen Hundred Course of Fire (1500)

The match is called the 1500 because there is a total of 150 rounds with each round having a possible score of 10, giving a maximum score of 1500. The match consists of 5 practices or series (usually called matches) firing from 10m to 50m. All series start with the handgun loaded and holstered. Once loaded and holstered, it is presumed that the competitor is ready.

Sitting is deemed to be both buttocks on the ground. No part of the handgun may touch the barricade or post.

Series 1	10m	Standing	12	Shots in 20 secs	
	15m	Standing	12	Shots in 20 secs	
Series 2	25m	Kneeling	6	Shots in 20 secs	Total
		Standing	6	Shots Left Hand	Time
		Standing	6	Shots Right Hand	90 secs
Series 3	50m	Sitting	6	Shots	Total
		Kneeling	6	Shots Barricade	Time
		Standing	6	Shots Left Hand Barricade	165
		Standing	6	Shots Right Hand Barricade	secs
Series 4	25m	Standing	12	Shots in 35 secs	
		Standing	12	Shots in 35 secs	
Series 5					
Stage 1	10m	Standing	12	Shots in 20 secs	
Stage 2	25m	Kneeling	6	Shots in 20 secs	Total
		Standing	6	Shots Left Hand Barricade	Time
		Standing	6	Shots Right Hand Barricade	90 secs
Stage 3	50m	Sitting	6	Shots	Total
		Kneeling	6	Shots Barricade	Time
		Standing	6	Shots Left Hand Barricade	165
		Standing	6	Shots Right Hand Barricade	secs
Stage 4	25m	Standing	6	Shots in 12 secs	

Total number of rounds fired from each position

Standing Unsupported	72	
Kneeling	24	12 may be fired using the barricade
Sitting	18	
Right Hand Barricade	18	
Left Hand Barricade	18	

	150	Highest Possible Score (HPS) is 1500

It will be seen from this that approximately 50% of practise should be carried out from the kneeling, sitting and barricade positions to confirm the HPA and POA. On ranges where the prone position is permitted the course of fire may be amended.

Bianchi Cup

This action shooting discipline, as with the 1500, originated in the USA and is run under the USA/NRA Action Pistol Shooting Rules. These rules state that in order to be eligible to compete, a competitor must successfully complete the Tyro Course or demonstrate equivalent proficiency to the satisfaction of the tournament officials.

In the USA competitors must have 70% of the highest possible score (HPS), ie 168 out of 240, and pass safety observations by officials to progress to the next level of the competition. Equipment must be inspected by officials for safety requirements.

The ready position to start is with the handgun holstered in a safe condition. Single action revolvers which are not fitted with a bar that transfers the blow of the hammer onto the firing pin, must have the hammer lowered onto an empty chamber.

Double action revolvers must also be holstered hammer down. Revolvers of modern manufacture which allow the hammer to be rested above a loaded cartridge may be used when loading with 6 rounds.

When using a single action semi automatic pistol the hammer must be fully down (not on the safety notch or half cock notch) for thumb cocking, to fire the first shot, or fully cocked with the safety catch applied. Double action pistols must not be holstered when cocked, if the safety mechanism lowers (de-cocks) the hammer when actuated.

Calibre
The minimum calibre of ammunition is .354 with a minimum power factor of 120.

Power Factor = Bullet Weight in grains x Velocity in feet per second ÷1000.

Accuracy
No advantage is gained by firing the required number of shots in a faster time than that which is permitted, or by using ammunition with a higher power factor (unless it is for greater efficiency when using a compensator).

Specific Rules for the Conduct of the Tyro Course Match

1. 3 x NRA, D1 (Bianchi) targets spaced 45" centre to centre. (This covers a 3 yd frontage).

2. Range 10 yds.

3. Ten points for hits in or touching the 8" circle line.
   Eight points for a hit in or touching the 12" circle line.
   5 points for a hit on the remainder of the target.

You also score an X for a hit in or touching the 4" circle line. In the event of a tie the winner is the one with the highest X count.

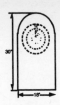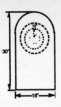

NRA (USA) D1 Target

Tyro Course of Fire

Stage 1
1. On the first exposure or signal, draw and fire 2 shots at the centre target in 5 seconds.

2. On the second exposure or signal, draw and fire 2 shots at the left target in 5 seconds.

3. On the third exposure or signal, draw and fire 2 shots on the right target in 5 seconds.

Stage 2
1. On the exposure or signal, draw and fire 2 shots at each target in 8 seconds.

Stage 3
1. On the exposure or signal, draw and fire 2 shots at each target, reload and fire 2 more shots at each target in 20 seconds.

Shot holes are easily seen. **The firer should not aim off for shots that fall within his HPA** as this will move the HPA in relation to the new POA. In any event, the firer should not focus on the shot holes as this will lead to an error in sight alignment.

On achieving the required standard, the firer can then go on to other courses of fire. Each one provides an interesting and progressive shooting programme. These include the:

Barricade Event
Moving Target Event (Modified)
Falling Plate Event
Speed Event (Man v Man)

Barricade Event

This course of fire consists of 4 stages with 2 strings of 6 shots in each string. 1 string is fired from the right hand side of the barricade at a single Bianchi target and 1 string from the left, after reloading if necessary.

Stage 1
1. 10 yds, 5 second exposure of the target, fire 6 shots from the right side of the barricade. (1st string of shots).

2. 10 yds, 5 second exposure of the target, fire 6 shots from the left side of the barricade. (2nd string of shots).

Stage 2
1. 15 yds, 6 second exposure of the target, fire 6 shots from the right side of the barricade. (1st string of shots).

2. 15 yds, 6 second exposure of the target, fire 6 shots from the left side of the barricade. (2nd string of shots).

Stage 3
1. 25 yds, 7 second exposure of the target, fire 6 shots from the right side of the barricade. (1st string of shots).

2. 25 yds, 7 second exposure of the target, fire 6 shots from the left side of the barricade. (2nd string of shots).

Stage 4
1. 35 yds, 8 second exposure of the target, fire 6 shots from the right side of the barricade. (1st string of shots).

2. 35 yds, 8 second exposure of the target, fire 6 shots from the left side of the barricade. (2nd string of shots).

In the National Championships, the time limit may be reduced by up to 2 seconds, for each string by the Match Director.

The barricade is 6 ft (1.8m) high by 2 ft (600 mm) wide. This is the width between the foot fault lines forming the sides of the shooting box, which is 3 ft (900 mm) long.

A penalty of 10 points is deducted for each shot fired when not behind the cover of the barricade. The barrel may be held against the side of the barricade to steady the revolver. It may be found that the MPI is displaced by the change in jump of the initial movement when firing.

Safety
It is unsafe to hold a revolver forward of the cylinder face. **The danger of personal injury should be seriously considered before holding the barrel or lug**, if fitted.

Moving Target Event (Modified)

This course of fire consists of 4 stages, with 2 strings of 6 shots. The Bianchi target moves across the range at 10 feet (3m) per sec (jogging speed) and is exposed between 2 barricades for 6 secs in each direction.

Stage 1

1. 10 yds, 6 shots, target moving right to left. (1st string of shots).

2. 10 yds, 6 shots, target moving left to right. (2nd string of shots).

Stage 2

1. 15 yds, 6 shots, target moving right to left. (1st string of shots).

2. 15 yds, 6 shots, target moving left to right. (2nd string of shots).

Stage 3

1. 20 yds, 3 shots, target moving right to left. (1st string of shots).
    20 yds, 3 shots, target moving left to right. (1st string of shots).

2. 20 yds, 3 shots, target moving right to left. (2nd string of shots).
    20 yds, 3 shots, target moving left to right. (2nd string of shots).

Stage 4

1. 25 yds, 3 shots, target moving right to left. (1st string of shots).
    25 yds, 3 shots, target moving left to right. (1st string of shots).

2. 25 yds, 3 shots, target moving right to left. (2nd string of shots).
    25 yds, 3 shots, target moving left to right. (2nd string of shots).

The start position for each string is with the handgun holstered and the hands raised to shoulder height. 10 points are deducted for each premature start, each procedural error, for example, firing more than the required number of shots in each string and for hitting the barricades at either end of the target run.

Moving Targets

On purpose built moving target ranges, which permit firing over a wide arc, the speed is variable, for example, 2m per second walking speed, 4m per second running speed.

Unfortunately, civilian gun clubs are not permitted to use this type of range as it is deemed to be inappropriate by the authorities for civilians to use combat type ranges. (This also includes electric target ranges, where targets fall when hit).

On certain gallery ranges it may be possible to engage a moving target between a number of lanes (this will be found in the range orders). A hand held target protrudes above the butt mantlet, moving at the required speed. (It will probably be found that firing is not permitted at ranges of less than 100 yds as the arc of fire and quadrant elevation will increase to greater than that permitted by the range orders). If the range orders state that Sub Machine Guns may be fired at less than 100m, it should be possible to apply for the orders to be amended to include handguns.

In the Bianchi Moving Target Event, the target moves 10 ft per second and is exposed for 6 seconds. The time of flight of the bullet is dependent on its velocity. Obviously a slow moving .45 ACP bullet has a longer time of flight than a 9 mm high velocity round when fired over the same distance.

In theory the amount of lead can be calculated from the velocity of the ammunition, the range to the target and the speed the target is moving.

This does not take into account the direction that the target is moving in, the effect of the drift of the bullet caused by the direction of the rifling twist or the loss of velocity as the bullet travels to the target. Neither does it take into consideration the lateral line of departure of the bullet as the muzzle is traversed to maintain the lead.

In practical terms, the amount of lead required to engage a target moving at 10 ft (3m) per second is:

Range	Lead Required	
10 yds	4"	from the centre of the target.
15 yds	6"	from the centre of the target.
20 yds	8"	from the centre of the target.
25 yds	10"	from the centre of the target.

As the target is only 18" (450 mm) wide this results in having to aim off the target at 25 yards in order to obtain the lead. Do not 'lose sight' by trying to focus on an imaginary aiming mark which does not exist. At 10 and 15 yards the lines of the 8" and 12" (4" and 6" radii) may be used as a point of aim. Also, when selecting a POA at 20 and 25 yards consider the effect of trajectory.

The firer should confirm during practise the lead required using his handgun and ammunition. There are now sights available which have lateral 'aim off' adjustments specifically designed for the moving target event.

Falling Plate Event

This course of fire consists of 4 stages, with 2 strings of 6 shots in each stage. The start position is with the handgun holstered with the hands held at shoulder height (surrender position), facing six 8" (200 mm) steel plates, 1 ft (300 mm) apart, 4 ft (1.2m) above ground level, to the bottom edge of the plates.

The signal to start each string is given after the commands 'Stand by' and 'Ready'. On receiving the signal, draw and engage each target with 1 shot. The target must fall when hit in order to score. (10 points).

A penalty of 10 points is deducted for a premature start, for firing more than the designated number of shots or for firing shots over time.

Stage 1
1. 10 yds, 6 shots in 6 seconds each string.

Stage 2
1. 15 yds, 6 shots in 7 seconds each string.

Stage 3
1. 20 yds, 6 shots in 8 seconds each string.

Stage 4
1. 25 yds, 6 shots in 9 seconds each string.

Safety
All distances, time and other information is approximate. The foregoing should be considered as a guideline only and is subject to change by the Tournament Sponsor if necessary, in the interests of safety, sportsmanship or other considerations.

Safety Considerations
In the UK, it is possible for Service Personnel to engage steel plates, (using 9 mm ammunition) which fall when hit at a minimum range of 25m, providing that it is permitted in range orders, as there will be some backsplash.

Non-military users must comply with the terms of their licence to use MOD ranges and the range safety certificate when using a club range. The licence and certificate usually include restrictions. These usually state that non-penetrable targets are not permitted, (there are exceptions, for example, at Bisley) and that the minimum range is 10m (32'6") with the exception of the police who may fire from 7m (23 ft)at paper targets.

Arc of Fire
On ranges that have a limited arc of fire (in each lane) the firer can move laterally along the firing line into designated boxes, (firing points), providing the handgun is in a safe condition. (Hammer down or safety mechanism activated).

Distance Between Firer
The minimum distance between firers is normally 1.8m (6 ft) in order to protect adjacent firers, the coach and spotter, from ejected cases from a pistol or side blast from a revolver. This distance may be reduced to 1m between firers provided that screens are in place.

Reactive Targets

These targets, which fall when hit, do not present a ricochet or backsplash hazard and can quickly be assembled using a Bianchi target with the centre cut out of it to the required size. An inflated balloon is inserted into the hole.

Reactive Target

The backing target is stapled to a post with the scoring centre cut out. This hole can be 4", 8" or 12" diameter depending on the range or the standard of the firers' shooting ability. The facing target is attached at the bottom edge with masking tape to form a hinge.

Insert the inflated balloon through both apertures, allowing the face target to lie slightly forward to enable it to fall when the balloon is hit.

Man v Man

This can be quickly set up and run using reactive targets. The 2 middle targets are hinged at an angle to overlap. This confirms the winner as the bottom target was the first one hit in a close match.

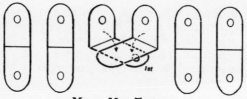

Man v Man Targets

Procedure
Firers hands touching ear defenders. Tyros (firers who are new to the discipline) should start from the alert position.

On the signal to start, draw and engage targets tactically (nearest first).

Winner
The winner of each stage is the firer who, in the quickest time, drops his targets before his opponent.

Squadding
Numbers are drawn on the range with odd numbers on the left and even numbers on the right.

Man v Man Target Layout

Duelling competitions, using single shot pistols, may be organised with each pair only permitted to fire 1 shot. (In the event of the target not falling, it may be scored to decide the winner).

Similarly, fast draw competitions may be organised for vintage and reproduction revolvers associated with that era, firing single handed only. (Tyros start in the alert position, hammer down on an empty chamber).

The Speed Association (UK)

The Association has introduced penetrable, reactive targets for use in their courses of fire. These targets are ideally suited for indoor ranges and for use on a calm day outdoors. The targets and equipment are available from the Association.

Grading and Qualifications

Only matches sanctioned and publicised by the Speed Association will count as grading competitions.

All speed plate challenge events may be shot by any person, irrespective of membership of the Association. Only members will receive a placing and be eligible for prizes.

Only persons who have passed a Speed Association recognised course will be allowed to shoot in a class other than Tyro.

Grading will be calculated on the average of the last three available graded competition results.

Western Action Shooting

In the USA the Single Action Shooting Society (SASS) have published the rules for Western type shooting. These rules form the basis for the British Western Shooting Society (BWSS) courses of fire.

The history of Western shooting may be traced back to the mountain men, who came down to the 'end of trail rendezvous' to trade goods and to compete in shooting competitions. These meetings later evolved into turkey shoots, in which the firer had to hit the head of the bird appearing over a log, to win the prize.

As the West became more civilised, paper and metal targets were used in competitions to determine the marksmen. Prizes included Winchester rifles and Colt revolvers, which were the most popular during this era.

When Western shooting became a recreational sport in the USA during the 1950s, Colt reproduced their single action model of 1873 for use in fast draw events. Wax bullets were used against targets at short ranges. This model encouraged other firearms manufacturers to produce similar revolvers.

These 'Leather Slapping' competitions, using unmodified handguns, enabled firers to compete on an equal basis. They were the start of practical pistol shooting as we know it today. Similarly, there are different classifications for handguns and their modern replicas associated with the era, with adjustable sights - as well as different classifications for rifles, shotguns and derringers.

Single action Western shooting is generally considered to be fired with one hand as the other hand was deemed to be holding the reins of a horse or a sabre, etc. The BWSS rules include the following categories:

Traditional   using Both Hands
Duellist   using One Hand
Frontier   Black Powder

Colt 44 - 40 Revolver

The Colt Single Action Army Civilian Model is the most popular choice for Western shooting, due to its balance and natural pointing characteristics of the grip and the ease of cocking. The 4³/₄" barrel is also faster to clear from the leather than the longer barrelled models. When drawing from the holster, the joint of the thumb should be placed over the hammer spur to securely grasp it, cocking it back as the revolver is 'punched' forward quickly to align the sights before releasing the shot.

Safety

Using the pad of the thumb to cock the hammer when coming up into the aim may result in 'slipping' the hammer, thus firing. This technique was sometimes used for trick shooting with blanks or low velocity wax ammunition. It is not a recommended technique as there is insufficient time for the thumb to obtain a firm hold on the grip before the shot is fired and it is also probable that the firer will be disqualified from the match.

Revolvers which have been 'worked on' to slip the hammer will possibly have had the spur lowered (similar to a Colt Bisley model) and the checkering polished smooth. Removing the halfcock/safety notch and trigger to fan the action is not in the spirit of the sport and is a dangerous practice! The firer will be disqualified.

On military ranges, the range orders may state that handguns may be fired by sense of direction. **In the author's opinion this is unsafe and impractical even when using a Deringer at short range.**

Deringer

Henry Deringer manufactured cap and ball single shot pistols before the civil war, one of which was used to assassinate President Lincoln in 1865. He also produced a metallic cartridge model during the war and later manufactured copies of the Smith & Wesson Tip Up Revolvers before the trade mark 'Deringer' was acquired by Colt.

The name 'Derringer', spelt with two 'R's, was commonly used to refer to other easily concealed vest pocket pistols. The double barrel over and under Remington Derringer and the Colt single shot Deringers, which were often carried in pairs, were the most popular models. Apart from the double barrels, these were of similar appearance, with their bird's head grips and sheathed triggers.

American Double Derringer

This Derringer is of modern manufacture and is produced in a number of centre fire calibres, including .45, .44 Magnum and .38 Special.

Accuracy is confined to close range by the short sight base and the small grip/trigger design.

Lever Action Rifles

The tubular magazine can be re-charged quickly, by leaving the base of the previous fed cartridge protruding out of the loading gate to prevent it from closing until the last round is pushed in fully. Re-charging the magazine should be carried out between exposures of the target or between exposures of yourself from the simulated threat.

Winchester .45 - 70 Rifle (showing action open on lowering the lever)

The butt should remain in the shoulder during rapid firing/manipulating the action. Lowering the butt during loading may result in raising the line of bore above the quadrant elevation.

Winchester Model 1873 Sporting Rifle

Winchester Pump Action Shotgun Receiver and Fore-end

Safety

Fitting a trigger tripping device to the inside of the trigger guard of a lever action rifle, to permit it to be fired as the action is closed, is considered to be trick shooting and a dangerous practice, as is holding back the trigger on a pump action shotgun to rapid fire before recovering from the recoil of the previous shot.

Cap and Ball Revolvers

The practise of raising the muzzle up to allow spent caps to fall clear of the hammer recess raises the Line of Bore above the Quadrant Elevation. This can result in the firer being disqualified from the match and being banned from the range for unsafe conduct by a Range Conducting Officer who is not familiar with the technique.

A safer technique that also allows fragments of cap that are trapped between the hammer and the rear of the recoil shield to fall clear is to rotate the wrist inwards and cock the hammer underhand.

Safety

Pre-charged and capped cylinders should not be carried on the range or kept on the person, as fumbling and dropping it from a pouch or pocket can result in serious injury.

Smith & Wesson Top Loading Revolvers have the edge in speed against the Colt when loading and unloading the full cylinder. To even the odds for competitors using Colt type revolvers, reloading is seldom required during a stage. In stages where more than 5 shots are required a second gun may be used.

Smith & Wesson Tip Up Pocket Revolvers, Derringers and double barrelled shotguns are designed to be used at close range. It would be impractical to reload them during the exposure time of the simulated threat in the event of not hitting the targets.

Loading and unloading should be practised with snap caps during weapon handling practise prior to live firing until they become instinctive.

The manufacturer's literature should be complied with regarding the number of rounds that should be loaded and the condition in which the weapon can be safely carried on the range.

Practical Pistol

Practical Pistol evolved as a sport from the belief that the measure of a man's proficiency with a handgun should be through a combination of stopping power, speed of engagement and accuracy at practical ranges.

All three are judged equally, the winner being the firer who, in the fastest time, hits his opponent (target) in a vital area to stop the encounter. (The dictionary defines an 'encounter' as: meet unexpectedly, meet in conflict, be faced with difficulty).

Missing, not hitting a vital area or hitting a hostage or 'no shoot' target, results in being downgraded.

In service and police disciplines, the length of time the targets are exposed has been determined in relation to the range, changing positions and the number of shots to be fired.

In practical shooting, targets have to be engaged as quickly as possible in order to end the simulated threat. The exposure time of the firer is dependent on his speed, accuracy and stopping power of his ammunition.

Speed of Engagement
Drawing the pistol and adopting the position to quickly point naturally at the target can be attained through constant practise until it becomes instinctive.

Accuracy
This can only be consistently achieved by obtaining the correct sight picture. This can never become instinctive, although with practise it can be speeded up.

Sight Picture
Whilst it may be considered accurate enough using 'pointability' and a 'flash' sight picture to hit a man size target at short ranges, it becomes impractical at longer ranges, especially when the scoring area is further reduced by simulated non-penetrable cover or hostage targets.

Stopping Power
This is dependent on two factors: the ammunition and the placement of the shot.

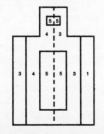

Calibre	
Major	Minor
.375 Mag	9 mm Para
.38 Super	
.40	
.45	
9 mm Major	
10 mm	

Value of Hits

Ammunition with a power factor above 175 scores major 5, 4, 3. Ammunition with a power factor between 125 - 175 scores minor 5, 3, 1.

Value of Hits versus Power

When using minor calibre rounds, the shortfall in power can only be matched by an increase in accuracy, which is usually at the expense of speed.

Whilst Practical Pistol has no laid down 'Course of Fire', as this is deemed to be impractical, certain 'standards' are fired. They should be attained before moving onto advanced stages, ie draw and engage targets at various ranges within a period of seconds. (Only individuals who have completed a UKPSA recognised course are permitted to draw from the holster in UKPSA matches).

Bobber Target

This type of target is frequently used in Practical Pistol competitions. The target 'bobs' out from behind cover and the amount of exposure reduces each time.

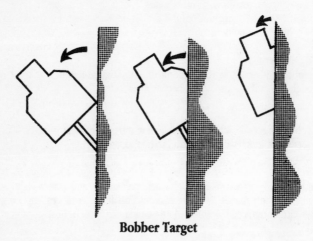

Bobber Target

Draw

This is a series of actions that have to be consciously thought through. It should be practised 'dry' with an unloaded pistol until the grip is consistent each time the hand comes into contact with the backstrap. As the pistol is drawn out of the holster, the trigger finger must be laid along the side of the frame until the barrel is parallel to the ground, pointing down range. As the arms are extended to come up into the aim, the safety catch can be dis-engaged, allowing the shot to be released when you have obtained the sight picture, whilst controlling breathing.

Single action pistols which have a frame mounted safety catch (that can be quickly dis-engaged without altering the grip) and safe action designs, where the safety mechanism is released by taking up the first pressure on the trigger, are more popular than double action designs. This is because a double action design requires a heavier trigger pull for the first shot or alternatively it has to be thumb cocked to fire single action.

Firing double action on the first shot, then firing single action for a double top does not offer consistency.

Courses of Fire

They should be designed to present the firer with realistic targets at practical ranges and with tactical situations (use of cover, etc) to encourage firing from other positions, for example, kneeling, sitting, prone, etc.

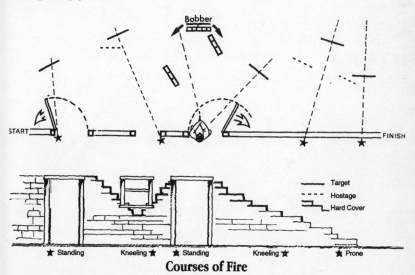

Courses of Fire

Procedural Errors

These can be the following: not using cover, foot fault lines and not engaging targets tactically (ie nearest first or tactically those posing the greatest threat), which results in losing practicality. Range officers should deduct points for each error, as failure to do this encourages the firer to expose himself in doorways, etc, or run through the course of fire, ignoring cover, which results in the firer being accused of 'Coursemanship' or unsporting behaviour, etc.

Time Deducting Points
Ideally, the time required to move tactically should not place the practical shooter at a disadvantage.

Match Conditions

This should ideally be designed as a surprise shoot, with the firer 'encountering' situations that are realistic, for example, targets appearing around cover as the firer moves along the firing line or pull-up targets and movers. Allowing competitors to walk through a course of fire, testing positions before shooting, is not practical and brings the discipline into disrepute.

A high standard of gun handling is required as the firer may fire from every conceivable position. 'No Shoot' targets (hostage targets) or simulated non-penetrable cover can be used to restrict the arcs of fire.

When engaging moving targets or targets throughout a wide arc, bend the knee/s to align the upper body. Pivoting from the hips will turn an Isosceles stance into a Weaver and vice versa, thus shortening or lengthening the eye relief.

Handguns

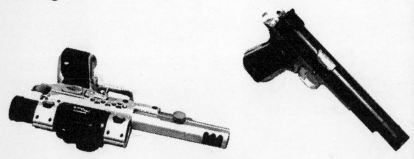

Practical Pistols

Practical Handguns have evolved into highly prized handguns with extended magazines, optical sights, compensators, etc. These resulted from competitors having a gunsmith improve the reliability, sights and handling characteristics of standard pistols to increase the rate of fire.

The devotees of Practical Pistol contend that the 'race gun' no longer represents the original concept of it being within the reach of the man in the street. This resulted in 3 Classes of competition:

Open Class Shoot

Optical sights, extended magazines and compensators are permitted. The holster may be worn in front of the hip.

Modified Class Shoot

The pistol has to fit into a standard box (the size of a Colt 1911 A1). The pistol may be compensated or ported. Optical sights are not permitted and magazines have to be the standard length. The holster is worn behind the hip.

Standard Class Shoot

This shoot permits enlarged safety catches, high visibility sights, replacement grips, checkering, etc. No compensator or porting is allowed. The holster is worn behind the hip.

Surprise Break

This is a term used in Practical Pistol to describe the firer being surprised (ie not anticipating recoil) when a shot is released.

To achieve this, the firer must know the amount of trigger pressure and travel required to squeeze off the shot. He must also ensure that his breathing is controlled and that the sight picture is correct on releasing the shot.

Constant practise is required to co-ordinate these essentials of good shooting so that the firer no longer has to think about them. It is at that time that he will have the confidence in his own ability to engage targets quickly and accurately within his HPA.

Practical Pistol is free style, with the firer selecting the position that the tactical situation dictates.

Firer Adopting Tactical Position

Courses of Fire

In Practical Pistol Shooting the firer is required to move, for example, in house clearing. This should only be attempted by firers who have attained the highest shooting and handling standards.

Safety Considerations in Practical Pistol

The safety catch must be applied when moving and the pistol must point down range, with the finger outside of the trigger guard.

Shooting Practise

Shooting practise should be carried out on various target profiles at practical ranges, within the firer's HPA.

Target Profiles

From this, the firer can confirm the practicality of firing from various ranges, using different positions and cadences of fire.

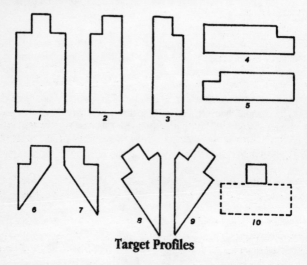

Target Profiles

Firing Positions

Drawing from the holster, firing around cover, engaging targets over a wide arc, etc, often results in having to modify the position.

From the previous illustration it can be seen that it is not always possible to adopt the ideal position, ie head upright. Ideally, the coach should have the firer practise in every conceivable position he is likely to encounter in competition, to confirm and record the POA and the HPA.

Engaging Moving Targets (Handguns)

The amount of aim off or lead, as it is usually called, is dependent on a number of factors:

1. The range to the target.

2. The speed that the target is moving.

3. The time of flight of the bullet.

4. The direction that the target is moving in relation to the drift of the bullet.

Example
If a running target (4 metres per second) at 20m requires the edge of the target to be the 'lead' in order to hit the centre, the lead required when engaging a walking target (2 metres per second) would probably be half.

When engaging movers, the standing position is recommended as it allows the firer the mobility to adjust his position. He is not restricted by the ground/body contact of the kneeling, sitting or prone positions.

Tactically the moving target does not present a major threat to the firer due to its movement. Theoretically a static target has more chance of hitting you; this can be confirmed by you trying to engage a static target whilst you are moving laterally across the firing box on a field firing range. However, a moving target should be the first to be engaged in a competition as it will probably be exposed for the least time before it goes behind cover.

AFSAM Combat Shooting

In the United States Armed Forces Skill at Arms Meeting, (AFSAM), international service teams compete in rifle, shotgun and pistol matches. Competing nations are permitted to use their own service weapons; US issued or the equivalent commercial models.

US Service Rifle

The US Service Rifle is the Colt Armalite M-16. The burst and automatic fire capabilities may be removed and Trijicon, Elcon or Susat optical sights may be fitted. The service sling may be used as an aid to steadiness and may be used as a single point or a double point sling when attached to both swivels. Triggers are tested to ensure that the minimum trigger weight is 5.5 lbs.

US Service Shotguns

In the combat assault course match, Winchester and Remington pump action shotguns are used.

US Service Pistols

The match conditions state that the M-9 (Beretta 92F/FS) and the M-11 (Sigarms P-228) fitted with Trijicon night sights are the US service pistols. Competitors using commercial 92 F/FS pistols, which are not fitted with a slide capture kit, have a slide life of 1000 rounds. They must certify that their pistols have at least an 800 round remaining slide life before commencing firing at the meeting.

Safety
The slide capture kit in the M-9 Service Pistol, prevents the slide from flying off the rear of the frame, in the event of the slide being fractured, when using service ammunition, and possibly hitting the shooter in the face.

The Trijicon night sight has tritium dots inlaid into the front sight and on either side of the rear sight notch, providing 3 dot sight alignment for night shooting.

De-cocking Levers

The M-9/92F/FS has a slide mounted de-cocking lever. When activated, the hammer is allowed to fall safely as the firing pin is blocked from coming into contact with a round in the chamber.

The de-cocking lever may be activated before racking back the slide to feed a round into the chamber. This allows the hammer to go forward with the same momentum as the slide.

The M-11/P228 has a frame mounted de-cocking lever which can only be activated when the hammer is fully cocked. This is the condition of readiness of the pistol, after making ready by racking back the slide.

Safety

Lowering the hammer with the thumb, whilst squeezing the trigger, is a dangerous practise as it does not activate the firing pin block mechanism. This can result in a negligent discharge, should the thumb slip from the hammer, or result in the pistol being discharged, should it receive a blow or be dropped.

The L9 (9 mm Browning) British service pistol is single action only and has no de-cocking lever. The frame mounted safety catch can only be applied when the pistol is cocked. In the UK Service Pistol match, the pistol may only be holstered loaded; it is not made ready until it is drawn from the holster.

Weapons Control

Pistols are inspected for serviceability and to ensure that they meet service requirements, ie, no unauthorised modification. Triggers are tested for minimum trigger weight.

Pistol	Double Action	Single Action
M-9	9.6 lbs	4.1 lbs
M-11	9 lbs	4.25 lbs
L 9	Not Applicable	5 lbs

Range Commands

Range Commands	Weapon Condition/Remarks
Shooters move onto the ready line.	The weapon is holstered and the competitor has all the equipment required for the match. Magazines charged, ear defenders, shooting glasses, helmet, squadding card etc.
Shooters move onto the firing line.	After crossing the ready line, the competitor may not claim that he is not ready to start the match.
Block Officer, is the line ready?	Range safety staff check that ear defenders, shooting glasses and helmets are being worn.
The line is ready.	Providing the Block Officer has not raised his flag to indicate that a competitor is not ready, range staff and competitors are informed that the line is ready.
Match number and stage.	The conducting officer informs the competitors which target they are to engage in their lane and the number of rounds to be fired during the exposure time from the position ordered.

Draw Pistol.	M-9; the de-cocking lever is activated. No magazine in the pistol. The chamber is empty with the slide forward.
	M-11; no magazine in the pistol. The chamber is empty with the slide forward. The de-cocking lever is activated.
	L9; no magazine in the pistol. The chamber is empty with the slide forward. Hammer down.
Load.	Insert the magazine.
Action	Pull back the slide to the extent of its travel and release it to chamber a round from the magazine.
	L 9; apply the safety catch.
Instant.	M-9; disengage the de-cocking lever to fire the first shot double action.
	M-11; activate the de-cocking lever to fire the first shot double action.
	L 9; disengage the safety catch.
Watch Out, Watch Out.	On the appearance of the targets or the signal to start, commence firing.

Safety

It may be considered safe to take up the first pressure on the trigger to shorten the length of trigger travel and to ensure that the finger is correctly positioned. Attempting to partially raise the hammer on the M-9 and M-11 pistols to try to reduce the length of trigger pull to that of a single action pistol will probably result in a premature or negligent shot.

Fire.	Come up into the aim, commence firing.
Cease Firing.	Verbal or horn blast. (A late shot results in 5 points being deducted from the score on that target).
Unload, show clear.	M-9; the de-cocking lever is activated, the magazine is removed, the slide is held open and the chamber is empty.
	M-11; the magazine is removed, the slide is held open and the chamber is empty.
	L 9; the magazine is removed, the slide is held open and the chamber is empty.

Combat Pistol Targets

The scoring area rings on the US Fig.11 targets are a different size to those on the UK Fig. 11 target.

USA	UK	Score
4" Circle	3" Circle	5 Points
6" Circle	6" Circle	4 Points
8" Circle	12" Circle	3 Points
Hits on the remainder of target.		2 Points

Shots touching the line are awarded the higher score.

In Match 204 Individual Combat Pistol Stage 1 Anti Body Armour, the shooter has to engage 4 targets with 2 shots to the body and 1 shot to the head on each target. The head is defined as being the facial area, from the chin to the helmet brim.

A hit to the head scores 5 points. Excessive hits to the head, due to body shots going high, score 2 points. Missing the head results in losing the scores from all of the hits to the body on that target.

In Match 205 Combat Pistol/Shotgun Assault Course, the shooter has to engage various types of targets during 6 stages of fire. For example,

8" x 8" steel plates	painted green to match the background
4" circular steel plates	
Fig. 11 targets	4 ft high, 1 ft 6 " side, charging man
Fig. 12 targets	upper body and head
Fig.14 targets	Sniper Head target
Combat targets	similar to Practical Pistol target with rounded shoulders and head, painted green to match background
Friendly Forces target.	Medic, painted white with red cross

Courses of Fire

The courses of fire provide progressive shooting training through slow, timed and rapid fire stages, using the standing, kneeling, prone and barricade positions, firing with the left and right hand. The none firing hand may be used to support the pistol.

In each stage, the first shot is fired double action. Pistols that are issued to allied nations' armed forces may be used by the nation's teams, for example, Sig Sauer P226 (British Army) as issued to the SAS.

Match 201 Combat Pistol (Level 1)

Stage 1

Range	25 yds
Position	Standing
Targets	2 x Fig.11 (2 ft centres)
Timings	1 exposure of 12 minutes
Ammunition	1 magazine of 12 rounds
Procedure	On the command 'Fire', engage each target with 6 shots in 12 minutes.

Note: No spotting scopes are permitted.

Stage 2

Range	25 yds
Position	Standing
Targets	2 x Fig. 11
Timings	1 exposure of 45 seconds
Ammunition	1 magazine of 12 rounds
Procedure	On the command 'Fire', engage each target with 6 shots in 45 seconds.

Stage 3

Range	20 yds
Position	Standing to kneeling
Targets	2 x Fig. 11
Timings	1 exposure of 45 seconds
Ammunition	1 magazine of 12 rounds
Procedure	On the command 'Fire', adopt the kneeling position and engage each target with 6 shots in 45 seconds.

Note: Only one knee may be in contact with the ground.

Stage 4

Range	20 yds
Position	Standing barricade
Targets	2 x Fig. 11
Timings	1 exposure of 45 seconds
Ammunition	1 magazine of 12 rounds
Procedure	On the command 'Fire', adopt a strong hand side barricade stance and engage each target with 6 shots in 45 seconds.

Note: Keep within the foot fault line.
No part of the pistol may come into contact with the barricade post.
The hand, wrist or forearm of either arm must be in contact with the post as the shot is released.

Match 202 Combat Pistol (Level 2)

Stage 1

Range   50 yds
Position   Prone
Targets   2 x Fig. 11
Timings   1 exposure of 60 seconds
Ammunition   1 magazine of 12 rounds
Procedure   On the command 'Fire', engage each target with 6 shots in 60 seconds.

Note: The start position is prone.

Stage 2

Range   25yds
Position   Standing to kneeling
Targets   2 x Fig. 11
Timings   1 exposure of 20 seconds
Ammunition   1 magazine of 12 rounds
Procedure   On the command 'Fire', adopt the kneeling position and engage each target with 6 shots.

Note: Only one knee may be in contact with the ground.

Stage 3

Range   20 yds
Position   Standing barricade
Targets   2 x Fig. 11
Timings   1 exposure of 20 seconds
Ammunition   1 magazine of 12 rounds
Procedure   On the command 'Fire' adopt the standing barricade position and engage each target with 6 shots.

Note: Keep within the foot fault line.

Stage 4

Range   20 yds
Position   Standing
Targets   2 x Fig. 11
Timings   2 exposures of 7 seconds
Ammunition   1 magazine of 12 rounds
Procedure   On the command 'Fire', engage each target with 3 shots during each 7 seconds exposure; returning to the alert position between exposures.

Note: A minimum of 7 seconds between exposures.

Stage 5

Range	15 yds
Position	Standing
Targets	2 x Fig. 11
Timings	2 exposures of 10 seconds
Ammunition	1 magazine of 12 rounds
Procedure	During the first exposure, fire 6 shots in target 1. During the second exposure, fire 6 shots in target 2; returning to the alert position between exposures.

Note: A minimum of 7 seconds between exposures.

Stage 6

Range	15 yds
Position	Standing
Targets	2 x Fig. 11
Timings	3 exposures of 6 seconds
Ammunition	1 magazine of 12 rounds
Procedure	During the first exposure, fire 4 shots in target 1. During the second exposure, fire 4 shots in target 2, during the third exposure, fire 2 shots in each target.

Note: A minimum of 7 seconds between exposures.
The ammunition required for the Match is 72 rounds.
The highest possible score is 360 points.

Match 203 Combat Pistol (Level 3)

Stage 1

Range	25 yds
Position	Standing to kneeling to prone
Targets	2 x Fig. 11
Timings	1 exposure of 50 seconds
Ammunition	2 magazines of 12 rounds
Procedure	On the command 'Fire' or the appearance of the target, adopt the kneeling position and engage target 1 with 12 shots. Adopt the prone position, reload and engage target 2 with 12 shots, using the weak hand to fire the pistol.

Note: A charged magazine may be pre-positioned on the ground to reload with, after adopting the prone position.
The condition of the pistol, whilst changing position from kneeling to prone, is with the empty magazine out and the slide back. The empty magazine may be dropped to the ground.

Stage 2

Range	20 yds
Position	Standing barricade
Targets	2 x Fig. 11

Timings	3 exposures of 50 seconds
Ammunition	2 magazines of 12 rounds
Procedure	On the command 'Fire' or the appearance of the targets, engage target 2 with 12 shots from the right hand side of the barricade, using the right hand. Reload and engage target 1 with 12 shots from the left hand side of the barricade, using the left hand.

Note:	The non firing hand may be used to support the firing hand.
	No part of the pistol may come into contact with the barricade.
	The hand, wrist or forearm must be in contact with the barricade post during releasing of the shot.

Stage 3

Range	15yds
Position	Standing
Targets	4 x Fig. 11
Timings	1 exposure of 7 seconds, 1 of 6 seconds, 1 of 5 seconds and 1 of 4 seconds.
Ammunition	2 magazines of 12 rounds
Procedure	**1st exposure**, engage targets 1,2,3 and 4 with 1 shot on each target; firing from left to right then return to target 1 and re-engage it with 2 more shots.
	2nd exposure, engage targets 1,2,3 and 4 with 1 shot on each target; firing from left to right then return to target 1 and re-engage it with 2 more shots in 6 seconds.
	3rd exposure, engage targets 2, 3 and 4 with 2 shots in each, in 5 seconds.
	4th exposure, engage targets 2, 3 and 4 with 2 shots in each, in 4 seconds.

Note:	Reload after the second exposure.
	A minimum of 7 seconds between exposures.
	The ammunition requirement is 72 rounds.
	The highest possible score is 360 points.

Match 204 Combat Pistol Excellence in Competition

Stage 1	**Anti Body Armour**
Range	15 yds
Position	Standing
Targets	4 x Fig. 11
Timings	4 exposures of 4 seconds
Ammunition	1 magazine of 12 rounds
Procedure	**1st exposure**, engage target 1 with 2 shots to the body and 1 to the head, in that order.

2nd exposure, engage target 2 with 2 shots to the body and 1 to the head, in that order.

3rd exposure, engage target 3 with 2 shots to the body and 1 to the head, in that order.

4th exposure, engage target 4 with 2 shots to the body and 1 to the head, in that order.

Note: Missing the head results in losing the score from the body shots on that target. Excess hits to the head score 2 points.

Stage 2	**Multiple Target Engagement**
Range	15yds
Position	Standing
Targets	4 x Fig. 11
Timings	1 exposure of 7 seconds, 1 of 6 seconds, 1 of 5 seconds and 1 of 4 seconds
Ammunition	2 magazines of 12 rounds
Procedure	**1st exposure**, engage targets 1, 2, 3 and 4 with 1 shot on each target; firing from left to right then return to target 1 and re-engage it with 2 more shots.

2nd exposure, engage targets 1, 2, 3 and 4 with 1 shot on each target; firing from left to right then return to target 1 and re-engage it with 2 more shots in 6 seconds.

3rd exposure, engage targets 2, 3 and 4 with 2 shots in each, in 5 seconds.

4th exposure, engage targets 2, 3 and 4 with 2 shots in each, in 4 seconds.

Note: The ammunition requirement is 36 rounds for the match.
        The highest possible score is 180 points.

Match 205 Combat Pistol/Shotgun Assault Course

The match fired at the United States AFSAM in 1995 consisted of 6 stages, with stages 5 and 6 being surprise shoots. This involved the shooter not having the opportunity to see where and when shoot and no shoot targets would appear across a wide frontage.

In stages 1, 2, 3, 4 and 6, the M-9 and M-11 pistols had to be fired double action for the first shot, after drawing from the holster. (The M-11 had the advantage on speed as there is no safety device to manipulate after drawing from the holster).

Shooters using the L9 were required to draw and make ready, before commencing firing. (Taking into consideration that a single action shot can generally be fired more quickly and accurately than a double action shot, there was no significant difference in the time required to fire the first shot accurately between the M-11 and the L9).

Each competitor was issued with 66 rounds of 9 mm ball at the start of the match. Magazines could be charged with any number of rounds, up to the capacity of the magazine, for example:

M-9   15 + 1 in the chamber
M-11   12 + 1 in the chamber
L9   13

Note: Between stages, the M-9 and M-11 could also have a round in the chamber providing the de-cocking lever had been activated.

Stage 1
Range   7 ft
Start Position Sitting in front seat of vehicle
Targets   2 x Fig 12 targets with hostage targets between
Timings   6 seconds
Ammunition   Minimum of 6 rounds
Procedure   On appearance of the targets, move out of the vehicle, draw and engage each target with 3 shots in each target.

Stage 2
Range   10 - 20 yds
Position   See procedure
Targets   4 x Fig 11 targets and 2 x Fig 14 targets
Timings   25 seconds approximately
Ammunition   Minimum of 12 rounds
Procedure   On appearance of targets, advance down range to behind cover, draw and engage each target with 2 shots.

Stage 3
Range   15 yds
Position   See procedure
Targets   12 x 4" Steel Plates over a 6 ft frontage, (targets fall when hit)
Timings   25 seconds approximately
Ammunition   Minimum of 12 rounds
Procedure   After reloading and holstering, move down range to behind cover, draw and engage targets.

Stage 4
Range   20 yds
Position   See procedure
Targets   6 x 8" x 8" steel plates
Timings   25 Seconds approximately
Ammunition   Minimum of 6 rounds
Procedure   After reloading and holstering, move down range to behind cover, draw and engage targets. (The targets are concealed in scrubland).

Note: The targets will fall when hit providing that the point of impact is above the fulcrum point on the target.

Stage 5

Range	5 - 10 yds
Position	See procedure
Targets	3 x Fig 11 targets and 2 x Fig 12 targets
Timings	The targets appear in random order for approximately 1.5 seconds. The contact lasts approximately 30 seconds
Ammunition	5 cartridges
Procedure	The shooter, on advancing down range, 'finds' a loaded shotgun with the safety catch applied. On picking up the shotgun, the targets appear. No shoot targets also appear in the area.

Stage 6

Range	10 - 25 yds
Position	See procedure
Targets	4 x Fig 11 targets and 4 x Fig 12 targets
Timings	The targets appear in random order for approximately 1.5 seconds. The contact lasts approximately 30 seconds
Ammunition	Remainder of 66 rounds issued
Procedure	After applying the safety catch and laying down the empty shotgun, continue the advance into the wooded area and engage any targets with any number of rounds until they go down. Targets appear across a 30 ft frontage (including a target up a tree), no shoot targets appear in the area and partially obscure enemy targets approximately 1 second after they appear.

Scoring for the Match

5 points per hit.
5 points deducted for hits on friendly targets.

Match 206 Combat Pistol

Stage 1	**Night Fire**
Range	7 yds
Position	Standing
Targets	1 x Fig. 11
Timings	6 exposures of 4 seconds
Ammunition	1 magazine of 12 rounds
Procedure	During each exposure, engage the target with 2 shots.

Notes:	Pistols not fitted with night sights are fired by sense of direction; pointing at the centre of the target with both eyes open.
	Corrections for alignment are made from the flash sight picture seen during the muzzle flash from the first shot.

Stage 2

Range	5 yds
Position	Standing
Targets	2 x Fig. 11
Timings	1 exposure of 10 seconds, 1 of 8 seconds, 1 of 6 seconds and 1 of 4 seconds,
Ammunition	2 magazines of 12 rounds
Procedure	During each exposure, engage the target with 3 shots.

Note: Reload after the second exposure.
A minimum of 7 seconds between each exposure.
The ammunition requirement is 36 rounds for the match.
The highest possible score is 180 points.

National Match Pistol Excellence in Competition

Stage 1	**Slow Fire**
Range	50 yds
Position	Standing, grasping the pistol with one hand
Targets	1 x USA, NRA 50 yd Standard Pistol Target
Timings	2 x 5 shot strings in 10 minutes
Ammunition	2 magazines of 5 rounds (as issued)
Procedure	On command, 'Fire', fire 5 shots, reload and fire the second string of shots within the exposure time of 10 minutes.

Note: Using the service pistol as issued.

Stage 2	**Timed Fire**
Range	25yds
Position	Standing, one handed
Targets	1 x USA, NRA 25 yd Standard Pistol Target
Timings	2 exposures of 20 seconds
Ammunition	2 magazines of 5 rounds (as issued)
Procedure	2 strings of 5 shots, each of 20 seconds.

Note: Using the service pistol as issued.

Stage 3	**Rapid Fire**
Range	25yds
Position	Standing, one handed
Targets	1 x USA, NRA 25 yd Standard Pistol Target
Timings	2 exposures of 10 seconds
Ammunition	2 magazines of 5 rounds (as issued)
Procedure	2 strings of 5 shots, each of 10 seconds.

Note: Using the service pistol as issued.
Personal load carrying equipment (webbing) and helmet are not required for this match.

MPI and POA

In practise, individual shooters should confirm the Mean Point of Impact (MPI) of groups in each stage of each match.

From this, the individual's Point of Aim (POA) can be confirmed for changes in range, position and cadence of fire.

For example, the author's personal POA in the combat pistol matches are:

Prone left handed at 25 yds	the middle fingers.
Prone right handed at 50 yds	the bottom of the 5 ring.
Right hand barricade at 20 yds	the black patch on the back of the hand.
Left hand barricade at 20 yds	the bottom of the rifle (web of the hand).
Kneeling at 25 yds	bottom of the wrist.

USA Fig. 11 Target Centre

As mentioned previously, the scoring areas in the USA are different to those in the UK.

Note: the centre of the bull is approximately 25 mm low and 25 mm to the left in relation to the centre of the wrist. This needs to be taken into consideration when zeroing.

Long Range Pistol

The coach is often asked, 'What is the effective range of a handgun?' This can best be demonstrated by the discipline of Long Range Service Pistol (9 mm Browning). The competition is fired at 100 yds on a 'Wessex target and at 200 yds on a standard pistol target, 12" in diameter in the centre of a 6' screen.

Course of Fire

100 yds - 2 sighting shots, followed by 2 exposures of 30 seconds, 5 rounds at each exposure.

200 yds - 2 sighting shots and 10 rounds to count in 12 minutes.

The 2 sighting shots are to confirm the effect of trajectory, light, wind and the drift of the bullet in order to determine the aim off required. To compensate for the trajectory at longer ranges when using standard sights, it is necessary to select a point of aim above the target which is referred to as 'Holdover'.

To practise this discipline, use a Fig 11 target at 100m and a Fig 12 target on a 1200 mm screen at 200m, firing from the prone or fire trench position, resting the pistol butt on a sandbag. (The rules state that no part of the hand may be in front of the trigger guard).

In theory, a firer obtaining a 75 mm (3") group from a supported position at 25m should be able to contain his shots in a 600 mm (24") circle (HPA) at 200m.

Long range pistol shooters have proved it is feasible to engage targets at ranges that were previously considered to be rifle ranges, for example, 300m.

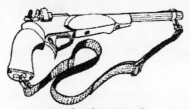

Single Shot Pistol

Shoulder Stock

Previous attempts to extend the range of handguns by fitting a detachable shoulder stock proved to be impracticable as the ability to hold the handgun more steadily is offset by the shortened eye relief, which does not present a good sight picture because the handgun sights were designed to be used at arms length.

Mauser Pistol with Shoulder Stock

Luger Pistol with Shoulder Stock

Browning Pistol with Shoulder Stock

Calico Pistol with Shoulder Stock and 50 Round Magazine

This pistol has been fitted with an optical sight and a laser beam sight to eliminate the short sight base problem when firing a pistol from the shoulder. The magazine can hold 50 rounds. The bag to catch the ejected empty cases can be seen underneath. The front bipod gives added stability when firing from the prone position. At the present time there are no matches available for this type of weapon, as there are for the Mauser, Luger and Browning, etc. The above was assembled in order to determine the practical long range accuracy of a pistol fitted with a shoulder stock, using an optical or laser sight.

Safety when using Pistols with Shoulder Stocks

When using a semi-automatic pistol fitted with a shoulder stock be aware of the working parts recoiling near to your face.

Development of Repeating Shoulder Held Firearms

Single Shot Rifles

Colt Side Hammer Revolving Rifle

Early attempts to produce flintlock repeating weapons were not successful. Neither was the Colt cap and ball rifle considered to be practical as the firer's supporting arm could be injured from spitting lead and burnt powder. In the event of a flashover between chambers, the result could be a multiple discharge, causing serious injury to the firer or bystander.

Colt Side Hammer Revolving Rifle

To reduce the risk of flashover, a conical bullet which has a greater bearing surface on the chamber wall may be loaded, instead of a round ball which only has a narrow bearing circumference. Ideally, lead should be shaved off the slightly oversized bullet or ball as it is rammed down with the loading lever onto the powder.

As an added precaution, the mouth of each chamber should be filled with grease before fitting the percussion caps. This also lubricates the projectile and makes cleaning the black powder fouling easier. To ensure a degree of accuracy and reliability, this type of firearm requires that the barrel is pulled through and the fouling removed from the moving parts after approximately 12 shots have been fired.

Safety: before charging the chambers with a powder flask, ensure that the previous charge has completely burnt out, or the flask may explode in the hand. Ideally, the chamber should be scrubbed out before reloading.

Smith & Wesson Lever Action Firearms

Smith & Wesson produced the first spring loaded tubular magazine repeating rifle and pistol. Both fired a hollow based bullet which contained the powder and primer. On firing, this caseless ammunition was fully combustible. This design prevented flashover, as the tubular magazine was below the barrel, although there was a risk of chain firing as the ammunition did not provide a gas tight seal at the breech or the primer could be struck by the nose of the round behind it, in the tubular magazine.

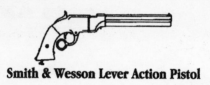

Smith & Wesson Lever Action Pistol

Note the attachment on the bottom of the butt for fitting a shoulder stock.

When Smith & Wesson sold the manufacturing rights, machinery and stock to the Volcanic Repeating Arms Company, Wesson remained for a period of time to supervise production. Smith, who also held shares in the new Company, left to continue with the development of the self contained metallic cartridge and to start their revolver business after obtaining the manufacturing rights for White's patent which was for a bored through cylinder.

When the Volcanic Arms Company ceased trading, Winchester, who was also a share holder, took over the Company assets and renamed it the New Haven Arms Company.

Henry, who had previously worked with Smith & Wesson, was employed by Winchester to improve the design of the lever action rifle. During this time, he developed the .44 rimfire cartridge and the mechanism to eject the spent cases from the rifle.

The New Haven Arms Company continued to sell existing Volcanic Arms rifles, pistols and new 10 shot cap and ball revolvers which they had produced under contract for the Walsh Fire Arms Company of New York.

These .31 calibre, double hammer revolvers had an elongated cylinder in which each of the five chambers were loaded with two combustible cartridges, a total of 10 shots. After cocking the hammers and firing the first shot, the trigger mechanism fired the charge in front. After releasing the trigger it was then squeezed again to fire the second shot, which fired the charge behind.

The Walsh Fire Arms Company also produced 12 shot .36 calibre revolvers. They were similar in appearance to Colt revolvers, apart from the 12 percussion cap nipples, double hammers and triggers. (These revolvers were used in the American Civil War).

Development of Repeating Shoulder Held Firearms

On completion of the contract to manufacture the .31 calibre revolvers, the New Haven Arms Company produced the Henry Patent Repeating Rifle.

Henry Repeating Rifle

As the .44 rimfire ammunition is no longer commercially available, the rifle may be classed as an antique and therefore kept without a firearms certificate.

An improved model of the Henry incorporated the King patented loading gate which enabled the rifle to be loaded through the brass frame (receiver), rather than through the tubular magazine. The Henry was then re-named the Winchester and was produced with an iron frame.

Henry Lever Action Rifle

Colt Revolver with Detachable Shoulder Stock

Colt continued to produce detachable shoulder stocks for his cap and ball revolvers. Although fitting a shoulder stock to a handgun enabled it to be held more steadily, little was gained in accuracy, due to the shortened eye relief. The weapon is fired with the butt supported on the palm of the hand to avoid placing it in front of the cylinder.

Butt Supported Position

Note the eye relief and the absence of eye protection **which should be worn**.

Winchester 73/76

Winchester continued to improve the design of his rifle to produce the first centre fire lever action rifle, the Model 1873 rifle. Selected rifles were finished to a high standard and fitted with an aperture rear sight and a set trigger to further improve the accuracy. These were designated 1 of 1000, of which only 124 were produced. Winchester advertised the Model 1876 rifle as 1 of 1000, of which only 50 were produced. Winchester also advertised the same Model 1876 rifle as 1 of 100, of which only 7 were produced.

Winchester 1873 (1 of 1000) Rifle

Winchester, who had previously purchased the Spencer Lever Action Rifle patents and stock to eliminate competition, was established as the major producer of repeating rifles.

Spencer Lever Action Rifle

With the continuing development of rimfire ammunition for use in full bore rifles, Spencer produced his lever action rifle. The tubular magazine was contained in the butt. Operating the lever ejected the empty case and fed a live round into the chamber. The hammer was then thumb cocked to fire.

Spencer Lever Action Rifle

Smith & Wesson Revolving Rifle Model 1880

Smith & Wesson, by fitting a detachable shoulder stock and a longer barrel, produced their revolving rifle, although less than 1000 of this model were produced.

Smith & Wesson Revolving Rifle

Marlin Lever Action Rifle

Marlin, who had previously been a sub-contractor in the firearms industry, started manufacturing his lever action rifle in the early 1880s.

Marlin Rifle

Colt also produced a lever action rifle which had been designed by Burgess. This was of similar appearance to the Winchester and Marlin. Production of the Colt Burgess rifle is said to have stopped in 1885, when Winchester mutually agreed not to start manufacturing revolvers.

Colt Lightning Full Bore Pump Action Rifle

Colt continued to manufacture a pump action rifle with a tubular magazine below the barrel. The full bore pump action rifle is not permitted in the UK.

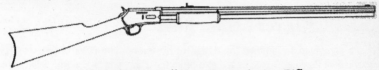

Colt Lightning Full Bore Pump Action Rifle

The author's has been de-activated.

Colt Lightning .22 Rimfire Rifle

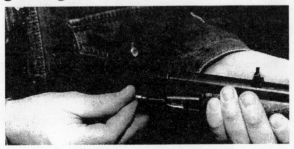

Colt Lightning .22 Rimfire Rifle

Used by the author for target shooting and vermin control. Note the Creedmore Aperture rear sight for target shooting and the Leaf Sporting sight.

Colt Rifle & Revolver

Winchester Lever Action Rifle

Winchester continued to improve the design of his lever action rifles to fire smokeless ammunition with Browning's patents and also produced a .22 pump action rifle, which, apart from the loading port in the receiver, was similar to the Lightning.

Winchester Rifle Factory Engraved with Gold Inlays

Browning developed a prototype self loading rifle that used the escaping gasses to operate the lever action on a Winchester rifle, as well as designing a self loading semi-automatic pistol for Colt.

By 1895, the Winchester Lever Action Rifle had evolved into a box magazine designed by Browning.

Winchester also produced the Lee designed box magazine, bolt action rifle. The hand guard which covered the top of the barrel was held in place by a barrel band, approximately 1 ft in front of the chamber. The swivel attached to the bottom of the band provided for the attachment of a single point sling.

The rifle evolved into the Lee Enfield and maintained its reputation for its smooth action and rate of fire.

Ammunition

Cartridge Identification

The identification of cartridges is often confusing to someone entering the sport.

Example	Explanation
45-70 - 500	This gives the calibre as 45 hundredths of an inch, with a powder charge of 70 grains and bullet weight of 500 grains. (There are 7000 grains in 1 lb and 15,435 grains in 1 Kg).
32-20	This gives the calibre and charge as .32" and 20 grains of powder.
30-06	This gives the calibre and year as .30" and 1906.
7.62 x 51	This gives the calibre in millimetres (7.62 mm) and the length of case in millimetres (51 mm).
308	This is the American Imperial designation for 7.62 x 51 ammunition.

Types of Ammunition (Nato Military Codes)

To identify the ammunition and to make it waterproof, the annulus around the primer socket is usually filled with a coloured lacquer. These colours can vary from country to country therefore the following information is intended for guidance only.

Type	Colour of Lacquer
Ball Ammunition	Purple
Tracer Ammunition	Red (and usually red tip on bullet. Increases barrel wear)
Armour Piercing	Green (and usually black tip on bullet)
Proof	Yellow (higher than normal charge)
Incendiary	Blue
Explosive	Black

The range orders state the type of ammunition that is permitted to be fired, which is usually ball ammunition only.

Reloading

Coating the base of the case with lacquer after reloading, in order to make it waterproof, may result in the empty case or live round hanging up and not being ejected. The case may be held tightly against the bolt face by the extractor claw, re-feeding it into the breech on closing the bolt and resulting in a negligent discharge (ND) when snapping off the action to ease springs.

Hang Fire

Military ammunition is normally primed with a cap which requires a heavy strike from the firing pin. A light strike can delay the ignition of the charge and this is known as a hang fire. When this occurs, the breech must not be opened for approximately 60 seconds (NRA recommendation). The ejected round should be placed to one side and retrieved on completion of firing.

Using thin primers with a heavy strike can result in a pierced cap, which causes a loss of velocity and possible erosion of the bolt face due by gas-cutting.

Bullet Types

Bullet Heads

Bullet types from left to right; Wadcutter, Round Nosed Lead, Semi-Wadcutter, Full Metal Jacket, Jacketed Soft Point and Jacketed Hollow Point.

The round nosed bullet, which is used in black powder, low velocity firearms, is cast from pure lead. This, with the original rimfire cases, prevented chain firing in the tubular magazine.

Round Nosed Bullet

When using centre fire ammunition in a tubular magazine, flat nosed or hollow point bullets should be used.

Flat Nosed Bullet

Hardened or jacketed bullets should be used in high velocity ammunition to prevent the lead being stripped off by the rifling.

Full Metal Jacketed Bullet

Full metal jacketed ammunition is designed for use in a box magazine. When using a rifle with a tubular magazine, only 1 round should be held in the magazine to prevent chain firing.

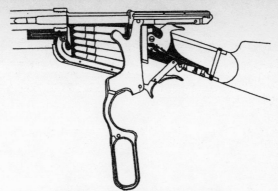

Winchester Box Magazine Rifle

Safety Considerations with Full Metal Jacketed Ammunition

When using this type of ammunition be aware of feeding or hard extraction problems as illustrated below.

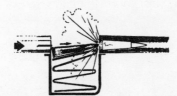

A Breech Explosion caused by a Double Feed

Rifle Marksmanship
Principles & Techniques

The essentials of marksmanship for the rifleman are similar to those of the handgunner. The main variations being in holding and aiming. Increased accuracy is achieved by firm body to ground contact and four points of contact in holding (the supporting hand, the firing hand, the shoulder and the flesh of the jowl).

The prone position is the most stable as the firer can achieve a tripod support: the points where the two elbows and rib cage come into contact with the ground form the base of a tripod.

Tripod Support

The elbows should not be too far apart otherwise the rifle would be supported using the arm muscles, rather than the bone structure. Neither should they be too close together or the position will become unstable. The position is correct when the firer is comfortable and has achieved the correct eye relief.

When firing from a bipod, the supporting hand may be placed under the stock to provide additional support.

Firing from a Bipod

A sock filled with sand may be placed under the butt of the stock to cushion the pulse and muscular tremors. Tightening or releasing the grasp on the sock will raise or lower the elevation of the barrel.

Sandbag Support

Modern sniper rifles are fitted with an adjustable butt spike for the same purpose.

L96 Rifle with Butt Spike (retracted)

The eye relief can be adjusted by moving the sight on its mount, by lengthening or shortening the butt, by adding or removing butt spacers, or by moving the body more or less oblique to the LOF. Once the rifle is sighted and zeroed, any readjustment of the scope position on its rail will change the eye relief and possibly the MPI.

The L96 Arctic Warfare (AW) rifle as issued to the military, has a green Parkerised barrel and green plastic stock. This can be changed to suit field conditions, for example, snow or sand etc.

The Police are issued with the Arctic Warfare Police (AWP) model which has been modified by extending the thumb hole grip and cut out in the stock to enable the magazines to be quickly removed. It has a black barrel and furniture and is made in various calibres, with rifling twist to suit the ammunition being used. For example, a 1 in 12 twist for 150 grain 7.62 NATO ammunition or a 1 in 10 twist for 168 grain 308 match ammunition.

AWP Rifle

Position and Hold

In the prone unsupported position the fore-end of the rifle should be supported on the palm of the hand without gripping. The grip with the firing hand and trigger finger placement must be consistent for each shot. The firer should pull the rifle back into the shoulder, which should be padded so as to cushion the effects of the heartbeat and shallow breathing.

Prone Unsupported Position

For a right handed firer; applying pressure with the thumb of the supporting hand will displace the shots to the right, whilst applying pressure with the fingers of the supporting hand will displace the shots to the left.

Snatching the trigger will pull the shot to the right whilst suddenly releasing it will displace it to the left.

Wearing a shooting glove, (mitt) discourages the firer from gripping and minimises pulse and muscular tremors. However, the trigger finger should be exposed when wearing gloves so as to enable the trigger pressure to be felt.

Head

This should be upright with the flesh of the jowl resting on the cheek piece to obtain the fourth point of contact. Any attempt to raise the head in anticipation of the felt recoil will result in losing the sight picture and allows the butt to 'kick' the firer in the face. This results in him becoming 'gun shy'. Recoil can be absorbed by the shoulder and the flesh of the jowl, providing that the position of the head is correct and there is no loose holding with the firing hand.

The position must also point naturally at the target without any undue physical effort (avoid using the muscles). Bending the right knee rolls the body over slightly and takes the weight off the stomach and chest, which assists breathing. This technique raises the shoulder to offer a better position to the butt and so enables the firer to keep his head upright, which maintains his balance and ensures that the pupil is central in the eye, rather than squinting and impeding his vision or having to cant the rifle.

Adjusting the Position

Natural Pointing (NP)

To confirm NP after adopting the position, raise the rifle up into the aim. If the sights are not on or near the POA then further bend or straighten the knee to adjust the position. (Do not move the elbows as this will disturb the tripod support and may alter the eye relief).

If NP is not achieved, the muscles that are attempting to hold the rifle on aim will either relax on releasing the shot (this is an involuntary action), displacing the MPI towards the naturally aligned position, or alternatively they will tense up. If tensing occurs the rifle will move in the direction that the muscles are tensing. The amount of the displacement of the shot will indicate the angle of error in NP.

The firers grouping standard is related to his ability to consistently obtain NP and the correct eye relief and will be seen in his mean grouping standard at 100m and his HPA at longer ranges.

The position should be oblique to the line of fire (LOF), enabling the supporting hand to reach the fore end and to obtain the correct eye relief. (Moving the body position more or less oblique to the LOF, lengthens or shortens the eye relief and changes the apparent size of the rear sight aperture/notch/lens).

Prone Unsupported Position - Front View

Using a Sling

A single point sling gives additional support to the forearm bone structure with less physical effort than a double point sling. When correctly used, which takes a considerable amount of practise, the sling gives stability and faster recovery from recoil. To adopt the position, the body should be more oblique to the line of fire with the supporting hand as near to the fore-end sling swivel as possible. The loop should be above the arm muscle with the end towards the forward sling swivel passing through on the inside of the wrist and over the back of the hand. Note the sling swivel in front of the magazine (omitted for clarity) in the following illustration.

Sling Swivel in Front of Magazine

Ideally, the loop should be broad and padded, to cushion the pulse rate, and held in place with a hook, button and flap, etc, so as to maintain consistency.

When using a double point sling, which is also attached to the lower butt of the rifle, the sling is positioned across the chest passing over the arm muscle through the inside of the wrist and over the hand. Because the sling passes across the chest, the breathing and the heartbeat may affect the stability of the rifle. Alternatively a sling swivel may be fitted in front of the magazine to eliminate the disturbance.

Single/Double Point Sling

Each technique requires that the length of the sling is adjusted correctly to provide a comfortable position. As with a change in position or moving the telescopic sight on its rail to lengthen or shorten the eye relief, the firer will need to confirm any displacement of his HPA when using the sling.

Safety - care should be taken not to raise the LOB above the QE when operating the bolt, as the RCO will consider this to be a dangerous practice.

Please note that the use of a telescopic sight does not actually make you shoot any better - it is simply that you can see the target more clearly; using a telescopic sight not only magnifies the image/target but also any tremors caused by the heartbeat/pulse or undue movement.

Eye Relief

This must be consistent for each shot to ensure that the apparent size of the rear sight notch/aperture is correct, and to protect the firer from injury from the sight during recoil. This is particularly important when using a scoped rifle to avoid 'sniper ring' caused by the rear of the scope cutting into the eyebrow.

Aperture Sight

The aperture sightsfitted to a service or target rifle increases the length of the sight base for precision shooting at longer ranges.

Aperture Rear Sight

This increase in accuracy is due to the firer being able to concentrate on the tip of the foresight in the centre of the rear sight aperture. The aperture sight increases the depth of field of view (length of focus) considerably. An aperture rear sight increases the sight base and makes aiming easier, as the eye no longer has to try to focus on the rear sight as it is attracted to the strongest source of light entering the centre of the aperture, providing that the eye relief is correct.

It is vitally important that the 'shortened' eye relief is consistent for each shot to ensure that the apparent size of the aperture is correct. This may be achieved by fitting an adjustable iris. Any error in sight alignment will increase in proportion to the sight base and range.

Open Sight

The rear sight on a 'sporting rifle' is normally forward of the chamber to lengthen the eye relief and is designed to permit an open field of view. This enables snap and fleeting targets to be engaged quickly at short ranges.

Rifle Marksmanship Principles & Techniques

When using open sights which are positioned well forward of the eye, the notch appears to be difficult to see, which is due to the firer trying to focus on two distant objects at one time, ie the rear sight and foresight. This is also the reason why it is impractical to use a long sight base on a handgun as the sights are too far apart for the eye to focus on both at the same time.

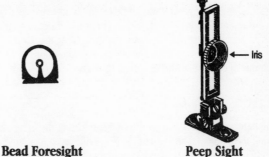

Bead Foresight   **Peep Sight**

Sight Alignment Error

It is vitally important that the tip of the foresight is in the centre of the rear sight aperture. When coming up into the aim, focus on the target and align the unfocused sight in the centre of the mass whilst taking up the first pressure on the trigger and controlling breathing. During the natural pause in breathing, change the focus to the tip and concentrate on it in the centre of the aperture (which should be now aligned with the centre of the unfocused target or the required POA if aiming off for a factor affecting the application of fire) and release the shot.

Example

A 0.5 mm alignment error over a 0.5m sight base (Sporting Sight) will displace the shot by 1 mm for every metre of range, therefore at 200m the shot would be displaced by 200 mm (8") and at 300m by 300 mm (12").

Breathing Control (Rifle)

In the prone position, breathing in will cause the barrel to fall, whilst breathing out will cause it to rise. This is because the rifle butt, which is in the shoulder, will move, whilst the elbows remain on the ground.

In the standing position, breathing in will cause the barrel to rise, whilst breathing out will cause it to fall. This is because both the arms and shoulder move together whilst breathing.

The effect of breathing must be minimised, for example, by aiming and firing during the pause in breathing.

Follow Through

It is physically impossible to release the shot without any disturbance to the lay of the rifle. As the bullet takes up the rifling the barrel starts to oscillate (vibrate on its axis). This is commonly called 'jump' and results in the bullet, on leaving the barrel, going high (which is called Positive) or low (which is called Negative). This, with any variation in the ammunition being used, makes it impossible to place all of the shots in a group through the same hole. A heavy 'bull barrel' not only minimises the 'jump' but also the felt recoil which follows.

Whilst breathing out, the first pressure should be taken up on the trigger. (**Warning**; not all weapons have this safety feature. This should be confirmed during dry firing practise). The pressure should be steadily increased to release the shot during the natural pause in breathing while concentrating on the sight picture. The Master Shot knows this and concentrates on co-ordinating the required controls by thinking them through.

Lock Time

This is the time between the pressure on the trigger releasing the firing mechanism and the firing pin striking the primer. The Lee Enfield No. 4 rifle has a lock time of 0.058 seconds. Some purpose built target rifles have significantly shorter lock times than this.

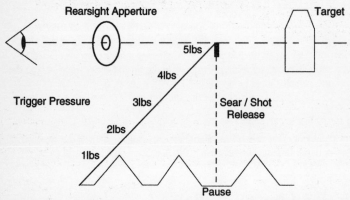

Co-ordinating the Sight Picture, Trigger Pressure and Breathing Control

To follow through correctly, the trigger should not be released until after the recoil, by which time the bullet will have left the barrel.

Summary

In summary, all that is required to become a proficient marksman is to co-ordinate the sight picture, trigger pressure and breathing control from a stable position, pointing naturally at the target and following through.

Providing that the marksmanship principals have been carried out correctly, the sights should land on or near the POA.

Practical Rifle

The practical range of the rifle is dependant on five factors which are: the sights, the rifle, the ammunition, the firer and the position used. These five do not include factors affecting the application of fire.

The sighting system on the rifle is obviously significant when engaging targets at longer ranges. A rifle fitted with sporting sights cannot be expected to shoot as accurately as a similar rifle fitted with an aperture sight   Similarly, it would be unrealistic to compete against a scoped rifle (other factors being equal).

Sight Base

The optical sight has the advantage in that the cross hairs (or pointer) and the target are both in focus (providing parallax and focusing adjustments have been made). It is vitally important to obtain the correct eye relief to avoid sniper ring, which is a half moon cut on the eyebrow. The position of the head must be upright to ensure that the eye is central with the lens. Any 'shadow' around the edge of the lens will displace the shot in the opposite direction.

Lens Shadows

The amount of displacement is dependent on the thickness of the shadow and the range to the target.

To overcome the disadvantage of 'loss of field of view' when using an aperture or optical sight, the weak eye should be opened between target exposures to open up the field of view. This also has the effect of resting the master eye.

Rifle Characteristics

The stock was originally designed so that the drop at the comb permitted the head to be positioned for the eye to be level with the iron sights. With the introduction of scoped sights, a cheek piece was fitted to raise the position of the head to the LOS and to maintain the 4th point of contact.

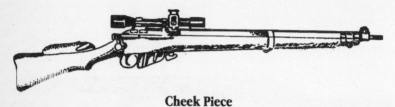

Cheek Piece

Stocks were later designed with a high comb that was sculptured to fit between the jaw bone and the cheek bone, to enable the effect of recoil to be cushioned by the flesh of the jowl. These are generally called Monte Carlo Stocks.

Monte Carlo Stock

With rifles of modern design, the stock has been raised in line with the bore to minimise the effect of recoil. (Pivoting the rifle upwards).

Barret .50" Calibre Rifle

The author with a Barret .50" calibre rifle showing the stock, optical sights and bipod stand. Note the size of the round held against the magazine. Neither the rifle nor the camouflage sniper jacket are generally considered appropriate for civilian disciplines, even though the jacket is designed specifically for shooting; ie padded shoulders and elbows with a hook for attachment of a sling.

Ammunition

In practical terms, the range (distance to target) for the type of rifle and ammunition may be classed as:

	Short Range 100m - 200m	Medium Range 300m - 400m	Long Range 500m - 600m
Lever Action (Rifle Ammunition)		√	
Lever Action (Pistol Ammunition)	√		
Bolt Action, open sights .223 (5.56 mm)		√	
Bolt Action, optical sights .223 (5.56 mm)			√
Bolt Action, open sights .308 (7.62 mm)		√	
Bolt Action, optical sights .308 (7.62 mm)			√

Rifleman

The rifleman's ability to apply the marksmanship principles is seen in his 5 shot grouping practises (at 100m). His hit probability area at longer ranges can be estimated from any displacement of the MPI of each group during the zeroing procedure or from the displacement of his groups when adopting various positions.

As with a handgun, the rifleman must have a sound knowledge of shooting. He must understand the theory of a group and confirm factors affecting his hit probability area. When this is achieved he will know at what range he can practically engage various targets and from which position. Whenever possible, fire 2 warmers into the bank (bullet catcher) or confirm the fall of the first (cold shot) at the start of each range day. This is particularly important if the rifle is to be used for deer stalking or vermin control which requires a first shot kill. The displacement may be caused by oil in the barrel, resulting in the shot going low or oil in the chamber which can result in the shot going as high as 150 mm (6") at 100m.

Other Positions

Kneeling

In the kneeling position, the firer can obtain tripod support by 'sitting' on the strong side foot and resting the supporting arm indent on the knee. (Do not rest the elbow bone on the kneecap as this is unstable).

Sitting

In the sitting position, the feet should be apart, to gain stability, with the elbows supported on the knees. The position should be oblique to the line of fire to permit the butt to fit correctly into the shoulder, and to ensure that the eye relief is consistent with that obtained in the prone position.

It will generally be found that the inexperienced firer's eye relief is lengthened when adopting other positions.

Sitting Position

In the above illustration it will be seen that the firers are dry firing (note the absence of ear defenders). They should also be wearing the clothes they would normally be shooting in as the thin summer shirts will shorten the eye relief and offer no protection to the elbows in the prone position. Firers should be coached to wear the same layers of clothing during dry firing, to maintain consistency in eye relief and placement of the butt in the shoulder. To achieve stability in the lying position, when firing at longer ranges without a tripod fitted, the Hawkins or the Reclined positions may be used.

Modified Hawkins Position

Adjust the body position to be more oblique to the LOF and grasp the rifle sling immediately below the forward sling swivel. (Keeping the arm outstretched to brace against the recoil). Rest the heel of the hand on the ground to support the rifle and place the butt in the crook of the arm. (Do not rest the butt on the ground as the stock may be damaged during recoil and it will also affect the initial jump).

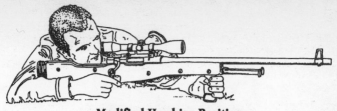

Modified Hawkins Position

As with any position or when using a sling, the POA/MOA should be confirmed during practise.

Reclined Position

Reclined Position

This position may be used by fitting a long eye relief (handgun) scope on to the rifle. Originally, an aperture rear sight was fitted to the end of the stock in front of the butt plate to extend the sight base. When using a rifle scope it will be found that the lens shadow around the circumference of the lens considerably reduces the apparent size of the aperture. To avoid the 'appearance' of a floating aperture, it is advisable to fire from a back / head supported position. The fore end of the rifle may be supported on the raised leg with the left hand placed on top of the butt to hold the rifle down into the shoulder.

Safety
Do not use this technique with a handgun because the short barrel may result in the foot being in front of the muzzle. Also, spitting lead, which is forced out of the gap between the cylinder face and forcing cone, may result in injury.

Standing Position

In the standing position, a modified tripod stance may be adopted by pointing the weak side foot at the target and positioning the instep of the strong side foot in line at a right angle to it approximately 450 mm (18") apart. This position gives stability to the front and rear, and to the left and right. When engaging moving targets or opportunity snap targets over a wide arc, bend the knees to align the upper body rather than moving the feet.

As the body is oblique to the line of fire (LOF), the right elbow may be raised in order to provide an 'indent' for the butt plate and to stop it slipping out of the shoulder. The le' elbow may be bent to allow the upper part of the left arm to come into contact with the side of the body, allowing the bone structure of the forearm to support the rifle rather than the muscle. The rifle is then supported by the fingers or palm of the hand on the receiver or magazine so as to lift the sights to eye level.

Standing Position

Engaging Moving Targets (Rifle)

The amount of aim off or lead, as it is usually called, is dependent on a number of factors:

1. The range to the target.

2. The speed that the target is moving.

3. The time of flight of the bullet.

4. The direction that the target is moving in relation to the drift of the bullet.

Example
The time of flight of a 7.62 mm (NATO) bullet to travel 100m is 0.1 seconds and to travel 400m is 0.9 seconds (and not 0.4 seconds - note the deceleration).

A walking target moves approximately 2m per second.

A jogging target moves approximately 3m per second.

A running target moves approximately 4m per second.

Lead (Theoretical)

Range	Walking		Jogging		Running	
100m	200 mm	(8")	350 mm	(14")	475 mm	(19")
200m	400 mm	(16")	675 mm	(27")	950 mm	(29")
300m	700 mm	(28")	1125 mm	(38")	1550 mm	(61")
400m	1000 mm	(39")	1575 mm	(62")	2150 mm	(84")
500m	1300 mm	(51")	2075 mm	(81")	2875 mm	(113")
600m	1600 mm	(63")	2600 mm	(102")	3625 mm	(145")

Rifle Marksmanship Principles & Techniques

Ambush Method (Calculated Shot)

To successfully engage a moving target using the calculation given in the previous table, the firer would need to know the precise time that the target was going to appear from behind cover, its speed and direction of movement to enable the shot to be released at a predetermined point along its path.

For example, at 600m, the lead required to engage a running target is shown as 3625 mm (12 ft 1") or approximately 10 target widths in front, to allow for the time of flight of the bullet to reach the target as it crosses the point (time of flight is 1.9 seconds for 7.62 mm NATO).

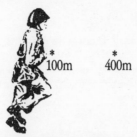

Fig 20 Moving Target - Lead

Representative Target

The actual width of a Fig 20 moving target is 375 mm (1' 3") across the chest area. The previously illustrated scaled down target (when positioned 2.5m away from the eye) represents the size of the target as seen with the naked eye at 100m or through a 6 x magnification rifle scope at a range of 600m.

The previous illustration shows the theoretical lead required when engaging a target moving at 2m per second (walking speed) at a range of 100m and 400m. This calculated amount of lead has been obtained from the target speed and the bullet time of flight and does not take into consideration other factors affecting the application of fire, for example, the direction of bullet drift, wind and movement of the target on the firer's reaction time, as will the other factors affecting the application of fire, such as light, trajectory, change in position, etc.

The lead should be confirmed during range practise by means of widths of the foresight or apparent target widths and this should be recorded in the firer's record book .

Swing Shooting Method

From the theory of a group, we know that the group size expands in direct proportion to the range. Similarly a sight alignment error will displace the shot in relation to the length of the sight base and the distance to the target.

The military use 'mils' as a unit of measurement. A 1 mil of angle change in azimuth (lateral bearing) of the line of bore (LOB) in relation to a line of sight (LOS) on the target, moves the mean point of impact (MPI) by 100 mm for each 100m of range fired.

For example, a 2 mils change in bearing moves the MPI by 200 mm when engaging a target at 100m. A 6 mils change in bearing moves the MPI by 3600 mm (12 ft) when engaging a target at 600m.

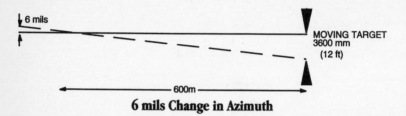

6 mils Change in Azimuth

It will be found during range practise that the lateral movement of the LOB in relation to an imaginary LOS to the target is minimal (1 to 6 mils) in order for the line of departure (LOD) of the bullet to strike the moving target.

Line of Departure

As the LOB is moving laterally when releasing the shot, the LOD is dependent on the lock time and the time it takes for the bullet to exit the muzzle.

Note: imagine the consequences of any undue movement during releasing the shot when engaging a static target.

Sporting Rifle (Running Deer)

This event is shot at Bisley using running deer targets. In reality no deer stalker would attempt to shoot at an animal on the move, because wounding is always to be avoided as it is considered cruel and unsporting.

Wind Effect

The effect of wind on the flight of the bullet needs to be carefully considered as it is often under estimated. It is a major factor affecting the fall of shot. The speed and direction of the wind at long ranges has a considerable effect on the flight of the bullet. Unlike the theory of a group or a zeroing error, the displacement is not in proportion to the range, due to the wind having a greater effect as the bullet loses its velocity during its time of flight.

To calculate the amount of aim off required, the strength, direction and range to the target need to be known.

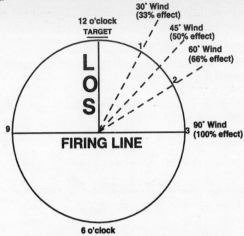

Wind Effect in Relation to Line of Sight

The wind has most effect when cutting across the line of flight of the bullet and least effect when in line with the flight of the bullet. The wind therefore has its maximum effect when at 90° to the LOS. As can be seen from the previous illustration, when at 60° (2 o'clock) it has 66% of effect.

Wind Strength

The strength of the wind may be estimated in miles per hour by dividing the number of degrees that the range flag is being lifted by the constant 4.

Wind Direction

The direction of the wind can also be estimated by the range flag using the clock ray method.

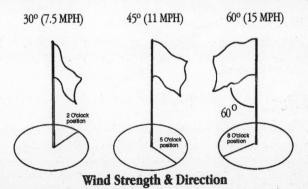

Wind Strength & Direction

Speed (mph)	=	Strength of Wind
5 to 10		Mild
10 to 15		Fresh
15 to 20		Strong

At 18 mph (72° flag), MOD Range Wardens are instructed to close the range because targets are likely to snap and equipment may be damaged.

When estimating the wind strength, consider the weight of rain on the flag and the uplift caused by the rise of the butts or mantlet.

Butt & Mantlet Flags

Calculating Wind Strength and Direction without a Flag

When it is not practical to use a range flag to estimate the direction and strength of the wind, for example when deer stalking; hold a piece of paper, grass, etc, out at arm's length, point it in the direction of the target and then drop it to the ground.

Calculating Wind Direction

The clock ray method may be used to estimate the direction the wind is blowing from. Point to where the paper first lands; the degree that it has been blown off line from the 12 o'clock position will give the direction of the wind, ie 40° or approximately 1.30 where its effect would be 50%.

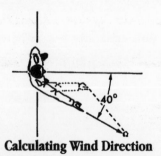

Calculating Wind Direction

Calculating Wind Speed or Strength

The number of degrees at which the arm is pointing away from the body when pointing at the paper may be used to estimate the wind strength by dividing by 4., similar to when using a flag. For example, 45° ÷ 4 = 11 mph (fresh wind).

Calculating Wind Speed or Strength

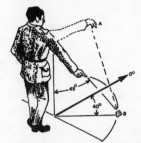

Combined Direction & Strength

Calculating Aim Off

To further illustrate the effect of the wind and to gain a degree of accuracy, the following formula may be used to calculate the required amount of aim off.

The Formula Consists of 3 Parts:

1   **To calculate aim off:**

Multiply the range (in metres) to the target by its first digit then divide by the constant 3.

The result is the amount of aim off in millimetres in a fresh wind blowing at 90° to the LOS.

For example - firing at a target 400m away,
400m x 4 = 1600 ÷ 3 = 533 mm aim off.

and firing at a target 300m away,
300m x 3 = 900 ÷ 3 = 300 mm aim off.

2   **To compensate for wind strength:**

In a mild wind, halve the amount of aim off, eg 300 mm ÷ 2 = 150 mm

In a strong wind, double the amount of aim off, eg 300 mm x 2 = 600 mm

3   **To compensate for wind direction:**

Reduce the amount of aim off for a 30° wind by 2/3, eg 600 mm - 66% = 200 mm

Reduce the amount of aim off for a 45° wind by 1/2, eg 600 mm - 50% = 300 mm

Reduce the amount of aim off for a 60° wind by 1/3, eg 600 mm - 33% = 400 mm

The formula may be used at ranges up to 900m when using high velocity ammunition, for example, 7.62 mm NATO.

The amount of aim off is from the centre of the target, remembering to aim off into the wind. Should it be necessary to aim off the target, use widths of the foresight blade or apparent widths of the target rather than trying to aim at a non existent POA which can result in not focusing on the sight alignment.

The firer should confirm by practise the amount of aim off required, using his rifle and ammunition at different ranges and in various wind conditions, recording them in his record book.

Minutes of Angle (MOA) - Sight Adjustment

It is feasible to calculate and adjust the sights by a number of clicks to avoid aiming off at some imaginary aiming point. For information, there are 360 degrees in a full circle and each degree is made up of 60 minutes.

Example

Step 1
600m x 6 = 3600 ÷ 3 = 1200 mm.

Step 2
No change for a fresh wind.

Step 3
1200 mm - 50% = 600 mm

Step 4
Assuming that adjusting the sights by 1 click = 1 minute of angle (MOA) and 1 MOA moves the MPI by 25 mm at 100m, then 1 click will move the MPI by 6 x 25 mm (150 mm) when engaging a target at 600m.

The amount of aim off required in a fresh wind blowing at 45° to the LOS when engaging a target at 600m is 600 mm (24 inches) from the centre of the target. Alternatively, instead of aiming off; adjust the sight by 4 clicks.

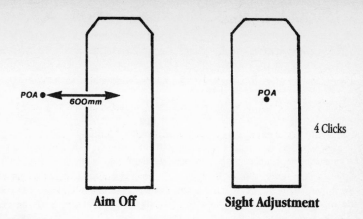

POA ●◄──────►
        600mm

POA
●

4 Clicks

Aim Off   **Sight Adjustment**

Spotting

The coach should observe the strike of shots that miss the target and should only recommend a correction for shots that are not within the firer's HPA. (A pulled shot is obviously ignored).

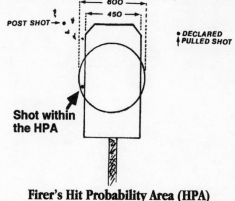

Firer's Hit Probability Area (HPA)

Shots that go wide of the target for no apparent reason may be the result of a shot being deflected by the target post. The coach may see the wood 'fly' when spotting with the scope.

Swirl

This is the displacement of air caused by the bullet in its flight and is similar in appearance to a vortex of water swirling down a plug hole. It is best picked up at the culminating point (CP) as the bullet is in the rise and fall of its trajectory.

The coach, by positioning himself behind the firer and observing above the line of sight with a scope, can pick up the swirl of the round in its flight and follow it to the fall of shot. With 7.62 mm NATO ammunition, the CP is approximately 200 mm above the Line of Sight (LOS) when engaging a target at 300m and 675 mm above the LOS at 500m.

Rifle Marksmanship Principles & Techniques

It is best seen on a warm calm day. The coach should use his thumb and forefinger to hold open his eye, to avoid blinking whilst spotting. An experienced swirl spotter can accurately spot the fall of shot to within 100 mm.

Mirage

Mirage is caused by the effect of heat waves (shimmering) in front of the target which distorts the line of sight to the target as rays of light are deflected. This usually results in shots going low. The firer should record changes in his POA / MOA for the effects of mirage and note the direction of any breeze that may not be apparent by other means (a breeze on a mirage has a similar appearance to water running in a stream). To simulate the effect of mirage when explaining it to a tyro; place a coin in a container of water and ask him to look from above whilst attempting to touch the centre of it with a cleaning rod or similar object. The light being refracted by the water will result in him missing the mark.

Competition Shooting

Competition Stress

This is normally called pressure, and has a similar effect to fear. This is usually caused by the firer being apprehensive about facing an opponent in a shoulder to shoulder match. Firers can be prepared during training to overcome this by using a Coach and Spotter.

Symptoms of Stress

The symptoms, which are self induced, cause the heartbeat and pulse rate to increase, usually resulting in losing concentration and speeding up shooting to relieve the pressure. In extreme cases, the firer will have difficulty in controlling breathing, will be sweating and will need to relieve the bladder immediately. In reality your scores are not being as closely observed as they were during coaching and spotting. It will also be found that when you relax your groups will be tighter.

Combating Pressure

Enter into competitions with the aim of achieving the average of the scores you produced in practise. This is the result you will be expected to achieve so don't be concerned; **shoot with confidence in your own ability.**

The entry fee is the cost of the personal experience and shooting knowledge gained.

Preparation Before Firing (Check List)

1. Weapon dry cleaned, sights blackened.
2. Ammunition clean and dry.
3. Speed loaders, magazines charged.
4. Belt, holster, pouches secured from movement.
5. Re-read the course of fire 'Think the shoot through'.
6. Check record card for POA/HPA.
7. Watch previous practises (Timings).
8. Ear defenders, safety glasses.
9. Relax and listen for the Range Officer's commands.
10. Be determined to beat the target. It is all that is standing between you mastering the pressure and containing your shots within your HPA.

To Confirm the Effects of Competition Pressure

Next time you practise try the following:

1. Do not obtain a firm stable position.
2. Do not achieve a consistent grip.
3. Do not obtain natural pointing.
4. Do not align the sights.
5. Do not ensure the eye relief is correct.
6. Do not control breathing.
7. Do not squeeze the trigger.
8. Do not recover from recoil.
9. Do not confirm POA and HPA. (After first stage).
10. Do not learn from errors.

- **Shooting knowledge can be obtained by Reading**
- **Mastering the techniques can be achieved by Practise**
- **Proficiency is measured in Competition**

Handgun Shooting Programme

Shooting skills can only be achieved through an interested and progressive shooting programme. Each stage must be mastered before going on to the next.

Serial	Activity	Range	Notes
1.	Range Safety Rules & Restrictions		Dry Training
2.	Handgun Familiarisation		Dry Training
3.	Marksmanship Techniques		Dry Training
4.	Grouping Practise	10m	Determine Grouping Standard
5.	Zeroing, Confirm HPA	10m	
6.	Confirm Theory of Group, Trajectory	15/20/25m	SPB Practices 1,2,3
7.	Confirm HPA/POA, Kneeling, Sitting	25m	SPA Practice 1
8.	Confirm Natural Alignment	20/15/10m	SPA Practices 2,3,4
9.	Confirm HPA/POA Left, Right Barricade	25m	PP2 Practice 3
10.	Rapid Practise, Confirm Cadence of Fire	10m	SPB Practice 4 PP2 Practice 1
11.	SPB Match Conditions	25-10m	Record Scores
12.	PPI Match Conditions	25/15/10m	Record Scores
13.	SPA Match Conditions	25-10m	Record Scores
14.	PP2 Match Conditions	50-10m	
15.	Bianchi Action Shooting Practice	10-50m	
16.	Practical Pistol Standard Practices	10m	From Alert Position
	6 Exposures of 1.4 Secs, 1 Shot each Exp		Standing
	6 Exposures of 2 Secs, 1 Shot each Exp		Strong Hand Only
	6 Exposures of 3 Secs, 1 Shot each Exp		Weak Hand Only
	6 Exposures of 4 Secs, 1 Shot each Exp		Kneeling
	6 Exposures of 5 Secs, 1 Shot each Exp		Sitting Record HPA/POA
17.	UK PSA Recognised Course		
18.	Action Speed Shoot		
19.	Long Range Pistol Practices		
20.	Competition Shooting		Club, Regional, National

Practical Rifle

Serial	Activity	Range	Notes
1.	Grouping Practice	100m	Determine grouping standard.
2.	Zeroing 4 x 5 round groups	100m	Confirm HPA
3.	Confirm theory of group	200m, 300m	Trajectory
4.	Confirm HPA, POA		
	Using sling		
	Standing, squatting	100m	
	Kneeling, sitting	100m, 200m	
	Prone supported	300m	Using bipod
	Prone unsupported	300m	
5.	Confirm the effect of wind/drift and light	300m, 400m, 500m, 600m	
6.	Confirm lead on walking and running targets		
7.	Determine the MOA (number of clicks) and record		

Range Work

The military require that the Range Conducting Officer and the Butts Officer be qualified or authorised. In the case of civilian clubs, the NRA is able to qualify individuals who pass their Range Officer's course (an experienced adult may act as the butts officer).

The Range Conducting Officer is responsible for informing range staff and competitors of the range rules and restrictions (which are found in the Range Orders) and ensuring that precautions are taken to prevent accidents to range users and the public. This can be achieved through a verbal briefing and by publishing a 'Range Detail', which can be forwarded with the competitors' Squadding Cards.

Ideally, the range staff should be briefed during the 'recce' on responsibilities. This will allow time for preparation and rehearsals.

Remember
When you sign for the range, you are declaring that you are qualified and that you have read the range orders and will comply with them.

In the case of military users, Pamphlet number 21 RANGE CONDUCT AND SAFETY RULES covers the general types of ranges found in the UK and Germany. Local Range Orders are to be complied with where they differ from those found in Pamphlet 21 in order to take local conditions into account. Similarly, changes in firing point procedure may be found when firing is conducted by a National Rifle Association (NRA) Range Conducting Officer (RCO). For example, in the event of the butt flag being raised during firing, military firers are informed to apply their safety catches and lay their rifles down on the ground pointing in the direction of the target, whereas civilian firers are told to unload.

The author strongly recommends anyone considering conducting range work to attend an RCO course for the appropriate discipline (rifle, pistol, moving target, black powder, etc), as it is in the interest of everyone to be fully aware of the responsibilities and possible liabilities.

Range Danger Area

The danger area is calculated to be the area into which a spent ricochet or splash back from the ground, mantlet or stop butt will travel, providing that the weapon is pointing in the direction of the target and the elevation of the line of bore (LOB) is no greater than 50 mils (2.8 degrees) in relation to the line of sight (LOS).

Should a negligent discharge occur with the LOB at a greater quadrant elevation (QE) than 50 mils, or when the weapon is not pointing within its lane, the shot will possibly fall outside the danger area. (A 7.62 mm Nato round will travel 4000m in free flight the length of the danger area on a gallery range is normally 2430m).

Placing target centres higher to that which is permitted by the range safety certificate will increase the QE. Placing targets at a greater distance apart will open up the arc of fire. Firing is usually restricted to the firer's own lane.

Range Conduct

No live firing can be 'guaranteed' to be completely safe. To ensure the safety of firers, spectators and the general public, properly defined range danger area limits must be applied as appropriate to the nature of the ammunition being used. The control of safety is the responsibility of the Range Conducting Officer (RCO) and the Safety Supervisors, as well as the firers, who must be proficient in weapon handling.

Notes for Range Officers and Safety Staff

Competitors

They expect the range to be run safely and efficiently. Firers have probably spent a considerable amount of time and money practising and travelling to the competition.

Rulings

Any ruling given must be based on the safety rules or the match conditions. The competitor is entitled to the benefit of doubt and if there are reasonable grounds, always decide in favour of the firer. For example, if 11 shot holes are in the bull (Practice 1, PP1) is it reasonable to assume that he has missed the target with 1 shot or is it possible that 2 shots have gone through the same hole?

Success of the Competition

This is dependent on the efficiency of the range staff and the integrity of the firer. In the 1500 match, firers have to show that all rounds have been struck in the cylinder before dumping. In Practical Pistol, no more than the 12 rounds should be fired at any target before it is scored and patched out as the firer may inadvertently believe that shots that have missed the target have gone through a hole in the A zone.

Protests

These are normally caused by short target exposures or bad firing point procedures, for example, the firers not being asked 'Is anyone not ready'? There are no allowances for malfunctions in the firer's equipment.

Re-Shoot

If any irregularity occurs which places the firer at a disadvantage, he is entitled to a re-shoot, for example, if the target does not turn fully.

Penalties

A competitor who is about to break a rule, for example, raising the LOB above 50 mils while operating the bolt, may be cautioned; so long as this caution does not include coaching as he is deemed to know the course of fire. It is probably better to remind every competitor of the course of fire before each stage of the shoot.

The firer should not be distracted from firing (by speaking to him) as he may protest. **This does not apply in the case of a dangerous practice**, such as loading, making ready before the order, not applying the safety catch or the weapon not pointing down the range, etc.

The firer is to be stopped immediately and ordered to unload. Close supervision is required at this time as the firer may fumble the drill.

Safety, Key Words

Do not use 'key words' on the firing point which may cause confusion, for example, the waiting detail may 'charge' their magazines or speed loader, however they cannot 'load' them. Imagine the consequences of an individual who may be down the range, scoring his target, being shot because you had asked a Tyro competitor, waiting in the next detail, if he had his magazine 'loaded' and was he 'ready' to 'fire'.

Watch Out! Watch Out!

Scoring

Competitors should not go forward of the inspection line. The range staff should only record the number and value of each hit and the competitor should sign the Squadding Card, confirming that he agrees with the value of each hit and not just a total which may have been miscalculated. The total score is completed at statistics.

Coursemanship

Distracting the firers should not be tolerated on the range. A competitor who continually claims he is not ready for no apparent reason should be stopped from firing and disqualified for disrupting the shoot, after first being warned.

Spectators and competitors who are waiting to shoot should not be allowed to distract the firers by rowdy behaviour. They should be asked to keep quiet or leave the range.

First Aid

A trained First Aider with a medical pack should be on the range during firing and the telephone number of the nearest doctor or emergency hospital should be at hand, so that they may be informed of the type of injury.

If the injury is caused by a firearms-related incident, the hospital will inform the police.

The Range Officer should record any orders he has given, such as 'Load and holster. Is anyone not ready?'; together with the action taken by the firer.

Safe shooting and may the best man or woman win

Future of the Sport

From the 1st of January 1997, civilian gun clubs will only be permitted to use Ministry of Defence (MOD) and Territorial Army Voluntary Reserve (TAVR) ranges providing the Range Conducting Officer is suitably qualified. The NRA also recommend that RCO's on club ranges should be qualified.

The Great British Target Shooting Federation (GBTSF) is at the present time advising the National Council for Vocational Qualifications (NCVQ) on the standards required in order to be awarded elements/units towards a professional qualification as a coach.

Individuals who produce evidence of approved prior achievement (APA) or demonstrate their proficiency to the satisfaction of the lead bodies' assessors or verifiers may be awarded a coaching qualification.

It is probable that only individuals who hold this qualification will be recognised as coaches. The author believes that it is also probable that NVQ elements and units will be introduced for firers at some future date and that coaches will be further required to have suitable assessing qualifications.

It is then possible that suitable qualifications will become a requirement when applying for a firearms certificate or variation, or when applying for club insurance.

Associations/Lead Bodies

The Associations from which to obtain further information on safety rules, courses of fire and membership are:

NRA   National Rifle Association,
Bisley Camp, Brookwood, Surrey, GU24 0PB, UK
Tel: 01483 797777

NPA   National Pistol Association
21 The Letchworth Gate Centre, Protea Way, Letchworth, Herts, SG6 1JT, UK
Tel: 01462 679887

UKPSA   United Kingdom Practical Shooting Association
P O Box 69, Southampton, SO9 7EQ, UK

ILRPSA   International Long Range Pistol Shooting Association
108 Sussex Road, Harrow, Middlesex, HA1 4NB, UK

BFAPA   British 1500 and Action Pistol Association
10 Southway, Eccles Precinct, Manchester, M30 0LJ, UK

TSA   The Speed Association (UK)
P O Box 11, Garforth, Leeds, LS26 8YB, UK

MLAGB   Muzzle Loaders Association of Great Britain
P O Box 493, Rhyl, Clwyd, LL18 5XG, UK

HBSA   Historical Breech Loading Small Arms Association
(for early cartridge revolvers and pistols)
Imperial War Museum, Lambeth Road, London, SE1 6HZ, UK
Tel: 0171 416 5270

SRA   Shooters Rights Association
P O Box 3, Cardigan, Dyfed, SA43 1BN, UK
(Northern Office: P O Box 357, Bradford, BD8 9EJ, UK)

BWSS   British Western Shooting Society
c/o Bob Dunkley Firearms
15a Hartington Road
Middlesborough
TS1 5ED
Tel: 01642 253333

Glossary

Following is a list of terms commonly used in shooting. It is not in alphabetical order as it is listed in logical order. It is not fully comprehensive.

String - The required number of rounds to be fired in a practice / series.

Run Dry - Ammunition expended / magazine empty.

Grouping Standard - Generally considered to be the size of a group achieved at the distance for which the firearm is zeroed.

MPI, Mean Point of Impact - The centre of the group.

ESA - Expected Scoring Area.

HPA, Hit Probability Area - The area into which a shot will fall at longer ranges after considering the factors affecting the application of fire., for example, change in position, wind, etc.

Application of Fire - The ability to apply the MPI onto the centre of the target from various positions and different conditions.

Zero - The precise point where the MPI coincides with the LOS at a predetermined range.

Zeroing - To move the MPI to strike the centre of the target in relation to the POA.

LOS, Line of Sight - The tip of the foresight level with the top of the rear sight and central on the POA.

POA, Point of Aim - The unfocused point on which the open sights are aligned.

Aiming Mark - The clear POA seen at close range with the naked eye or when using a telescopic sight at longer ranges.

LOB, Line of Bore - This is the lay of the barrel and the line of the departure of the bullet.

Azimuth - The bearing that the LOB is moved laterally in relation to the LOF.

LOF, Line of Fire - Pointing in the direction of the target.

LOD, Line of Departure - The line of departure of the bullet.

CP, Culminating Point - The maximum height to which the bullet rises in its trajectory. This is just over half the distance in its flight to the 2nd strike on the LOS.

Trajectory - The flight of the bullet which is dependent on the bullet weight, velocity and the elevation of the LOB.

Drift - The drift of the bullet caused by the rifling twist or the wind strength.

1st Graze - The point where the bullet first hits the ground, the face of the butt or the mantlet.

2nd Graze (Ricochet) - The second or subsequent graze of the bullet, the direction of which cannot be determined but is calculated to fall within the danger area, providing the QE of the LOB has not been raised above 50 mils.

QE, Quadrant Elevation - On level ranges the QE is the angle from the horizontal plane. On ranges where the ground rises or falls towards the target, the QE is the angle of the LOB raised above where it will be parallel to the ground. Note: on ranges where firearms are used which require the LOB to be raised in relation to the LOS in order to achieve the required trajectory, for example, black powder rifles, the range safety template will take into consideration this type of firearm and the calibre that may be fired. These can be found in the range orders.

Splash - Is the strike of the bullet against a non penetrable target (Steel Plate) or into the sand filled bullet catcher.

Backsplash - Separated jackets, fragments of lead deflected by the steel plates or previously fired bullets being hit in the bullet catcher, can result in fragments coming back towards the firer and is called backsplash.

Hammer Bite - This is when the hammer nips the web of skin between the thumb and index finger when firing a semi-automatic pistol.

MPH - Miles per Hour.

MOD - Ministry of Defence.

ND - Negligent Discharge.

Cadence of Fire - The controlled rate at which shots must be fired to meet the requirements of the course of fire, which is usually dictated by the target exposure time.

Angle of Sight - The angle between the LOS and the horizontal plane.

Striations - The marks on the bullet caused by the lands and grooves from the rifling.

Index

Order Form

✍ please complete this form (or a copy) and send it with payment to
S&S Systems, Bretton Court, Manor Road, Wales Village, Sheffield, S31 8PD, UK

Please send me ——————————————————————————————

Shooting Record Cards at £9.00 per 100 (1996 price so please check current price) ❑
    Number of cards required: ....   Total amount for cards: ....
    Delivery   Total amount for delivery: ....
    (UK delivery per 100 cards is £2.00, Overseas delivery per 100 cards is £3.50)

Additional copies of this book at £12.00 each (1996 price so please check current price) ❑
    Number of books required: ....   Total amount for books: ....
    Delivery   Total amount for delivery: ....
    (UK delivery per book is £3.00, Overseas delivery per book is £5.00)

                              Total Value of this order: £ ....

I may be interested in a series of videos to accompany this book. Please inform ❑
me of the details when available.

I am interested in personal coaching. Please contact me with details ❑

                        Type: Basic ❑   Intermediate ❑   Advanced ❑

I may be interested in future products or services applicable to shooting / coaching ❑
Please contact me with details when available. My interests are:

My details ——————————————————————————————

Name:
Address:

Tel: Fax:

Payment details ——————————————————————————————

Payment Method: ❑ Cheque   ❑ Cash (send by registered post)   ❑ Credit Card
                    (Please make cheque or cash payment in £ Pounds Sterling)
If paying by credit card, please complete the following:
Credit Card Details: ❑ Visa   ❑ Mastercharge   Expiry Date:
Number:
Issued in the Name of (PRINT):   Signature:
Address of Card Holder:

Notes

Shooting Record Card

Firer's Name: .... **Coach**: .... **Date**: ....

Firearm	❑ Handgun	❑ Rifle	Model:		

Ammunition Details and Load: ....

Discipline	❑ Service	❑ Police	❑ Practical	❑ Bianchi	❑ Rifle
	❑ Long Range Pistol		❑ Other...........................		
Stance	❑ Duelling	❑ Isosceles	❑ Weaver	❑ Tactical	❑ ....
Position	❑ Kneeling	❑ Sitting	❑ Prone	❑ Bipod	❑ Standing
	❑ Hawkins	❑ Reclined	❑ L/H Bar	❑ R/H Bar	❑ Lug/Stop
Range	❑ Metres	❑ Yards	❑ Location		
	❑ 10	❑ 15	❑ 20	❑ 25	❑ 35 ❑ 50
	❑ 100	❑ 200	❑ 300	❑ 400	❑ 500 ❑ 600
Target	❑ Static	❑ Walking	❑ Jogging	❑ Running	
Confirming	❑ MPI	❑ POA	❑ HPA	❑ Lead	❑ Group Size ......
Light	❑ Bright	❑ Dull	**Time**	.... am / pm	

Wind Strength (Speed)	❑ Mild 5-10 mph	❑ Fresh 10-15 mph	❑ Strong 15-20 mph	
Wind Bearing		❑ 30⁰	❑ 45⁰	❑ 60⁰ ❑ 90⁰
Wind Direction		❑ Left	❑ Right	
Rifling Twist/Drift		❑ Left	❑ Right	mm: ....

Sight Adj (No. of Clicks)   Left: .... Right: .... Up: .... Down: ....

Target

Notes

_____

_____

_____

_____

_____

_____

_____

_____

_____

_____

_____

_____

_____

_____

_____

_____

_____

_____

_____

_____

Shooting Record Card

Firer's Name: .... **Coach**: .... **Date**: ....

Firearm ❑ Handgun ❑ Rifle   Model: ....

Ammunition Details and Load: ....

Discipline	❑ Service	❑ Police	❑ Practical	❑ Bianchi	❑ Rifle
	❑ Long Range Pistol		❑ Other............		

Stance ❑ Duelling ❑ Isosceles ❑ Weaver ❑ Tactical ❑ ....

Position	❑ Kneeling	❑ Sitting	❑ Prone	❑ Bipod	❑ Standing
	❑ Hawkins	❑ Reclined	❑ L/H Bar	❑ R/H Bar	❑ Lug/Stop

Range	❑ Metres	❑ Yards	❑ Location			
	❑ 10	❑ 15	❑ 20	❑ 25	❑ 35	❑ 50
	❑ 100	❑ 200	❑ 300	❑ 400	❑ 500	❑ 600

Target ❑ Static ❑ Walking ❑ Jogging ❑ Running

Confirming ❑ MPI ❑ POA ❑ HPA ❑ Lead ❑ Group Size ......

Light ❑ Bright ❑ Dull **Time** .... am / pm

Wind Strength (Speed)	❑ Mild 5-10 mph	❑ Fresh 10-15 mph	❑ Strong 15-20 mph

Wind Bearing ❑ 30° ❑ 45° ❑ 60° ❑ 90°

Wind Direction ❑ Left ❑ Right

Rifling Twist/Drift ❑ Left ❑ Right mm: ....

Sight Adj (No. of Clicks) Left: .... Right: .... Up: .... Down: ....

Target

Notes

Shooting Record Card

Firer's Name: .... **Coach:** .... **Date:** ....

Firearm	❏ Handgun	❏ Rifle	Model: ....

Ammunition Details and Load: ....

Discipline
❏ Service ❏ Police ❏ Practical ❏ Bianchi ❏ Rifle
❏ Long Range Pistol ❏ Other..

Stance
❏ Duelling ❏ Isosceles ❏ Weaver ❏ Tactical ❏ ....

Position
❏ Kneeling ❏ Sitting ❏ Prone ❏ Bipod ❏ Standing
❏ Hawkins ❏ Reclined ❏ L/H Bar ❏ R/H Bar ❏ Lug/Stop

Range
❏ Metres ❏ Yards ❏ Location ....
❏ 10 ❏ 15 ❏ 20 ❏ 25 ❏ 35 ❏ 50
❏ 100 ❏ 200 ❏ 300 ❏ 400 ❏ 500 ❏ 600

Target
❏ Static ❏ Walking ❏ Jogging ❏ Running

Confirming
❏ MPI ❏ POA ❏ HPA ❏ Lead ❏ Group Size ....

Light
❏ Bright ❏ Dull **Time** .... am / pm

Wind Strength (Speed)
❏ Mild ❏ Fresh ❏ Strong
5-10 mph 10-15 mph 15-20 mph

Wind Bearing
❏ 30° ❏ 45° ❏ 60° ❏ 90°

Wind Direction
❏ Left ❏ Right

Rifling Twist/Drift
❏ Left ❏ Right mm: ....

Sight Adj (No. of Clicks)
Left: .... Right: .... Up: .... Down: ....

Target

Notes

Shooting Record Card

Firer's Name: .... Coach: .... Date: ....

| Firearm | ☐ Handgun ☐ Rifle | Model: .... |

Ammunition Details and Load: ....

| Discipline | ☐ Service | ☐ Police | ☐ Practical | ☐ Bianchi | ☐ Rifle |
| | ☐ Long Range Pistol | | ☐ Other...................................... | | |

| Stance | ☐ Duelling | ☐ Isosceles | ☐ Weaver | ☐ Tactical | ☐ .... |

| Position | ☐ Kneeling | ☐ Sitting | ☐ Prone | ☐ Bipod | ☐ Standing |
| | ☐ Hawkins | ☐ Reclined | ☐ L/H Bar | ☐ R/H Bar | ☐ Lug/Stop |

Range	☐ Metres	☐ Yards	☐ Location ....
	☐ 10	☐ 15	☐ 20	☐ 25	☐ 35	☐ 50
	☐ 100	☐ 200	☐ 300	☐ 400	☐ 500	☐ 600

| Target | ☐ Static | ☐ Walking | ☐ Jogging | ☐ Running |

| Confirming | ☐ MPI | ☐ POA | ☐ HPA | ☐ Lead | ☐ Group Size .... |

| Light | ☐ Bright | ☐ Dull | **Time** | .... am / pm |

| Wind Strength (Speed) | ☐ Mild 5-10 mph | ☐ Fresh 10-15 mph | ☐ Strong 15-20 mph |

| Wind Bearing | | ☐ 30° | ☐ 45° | ☐ 60° | ☐ 90° |

| Wind Direction | | ☐ Left | ☐ Right |

| Rifling Twist/Drift | | ☐ Left | ☐ Right | mm: .... |

Sight Adj (No. of Clicks)   Left: ....   Right: ....   Up: ....   Down: ....

Target

Notes

_____

_____

_____

_____

_____

_____

_____

_____

_____

_____

_____

_____

_____

_____

_____

_____

_____

_____

_____

_____

_____

Shooting Record Card

Firer's Name: .... **Coach**: .... **Date**: ....

Firearm	❏ Handgun	❏ Rifle	Model:		

Ammunition Details and Load: ....

Discipline	❏ Service	❏ Police	❏ Practical	❏ Bianchi	❏ Rifle
	❏ Long Range Pistol		❏ Other................		
Stance	❏ Duelling	❏ Isosceles	❏ Weaver	❏ Tactical	❏ ....
Position	❏ Kneeling	❏ Sitting	❏ Prone	❏ Bipod	❏ Standing
	❏ Hawkins	❏ Reclined	❏ L/H Bar	❏ R/H Bar	❏ Lug/Stop

Range	❏ Metres	❏ Yards	❏ Location			
	❏ 10	❏ 15	❏ 20	❏ 25	❏ 35	❏ 50
	❏ 100	❏ 200	❏ 300	❏ 400	❏ 500	❏ 600

Target	❏ Static	❏ Walking	❏ Jogging	❏ Running	
Confirming	❏ MPI	❏ POA	❏ HPA	❏ Lead	❏ Group Size ......
Light	❏ Bright	❏ Dull	**Time**	.... am / pm	

Wind Strength (Speed)	❏ Mild 5-10 mph	❏ Fresh 10-15 mph	❏ Strong 15-20 mph	
Wind Bearing		❏ 30⁰	❏ 45⁰	❏ 60⁰	❏ 90⁰
Wind Direction		❏ Left	❏ Right	
Rifling Twist/Drift		❏ Left	❏ Right	mm: ....

Sight Adj (No. of Clicks)   Left: ....   Right: ....   Up: ....   Down: ....

Target

Notes

_____

_____

_____

_____

_____

_____

_____

_____

_____

_____

_____

_____

_____

_____

_____

_____

_____

_____

_____

_____